Eat healthy, live happy and stay sane for the whole school year . . .

LAURA KEOGH · CERI MARSH

PHOTOGRAPHY BY MAYA VISNYEI

THE
SCHOOL
YEAR
SURVIVAL
COOKBOOK

HEALTHY RECIPES AND
SANITY-SAVING STRATEGIES
FOR EVERY FAMILY AND EVERY MEAL

(EVEN SNACKS)

appetite
by RANDOM HOUSE

Appetite by Random House® and colophon are registered trademarks of Penguin Random House LLC.

Library and Archives of Canada Cataloguing in Publication is available upon request.

ISBN: 978-0-14-753029-5
eBook ISBN: 978-0-14-753030-1

Editor: Bhavna Chauhan
Food stylist: David Grenier
Prop stylist: Catherine Doherty

Printed and bound in China

Published in Canada by Appetite by Random House®,
a division of Penguin Random House Canada Limited

www.penguinrandomhouse.ca

10 9 8 7 6 5 4

appetite
by RANDOM HOUSE

Penguin
Random
House

For Scarlett,
Esme and Julian,
the reasons for
all those lunches.

Contents

INTRODUCTION

As you can tell from its name, this cookbook is all about helping parents manage feeding their families through the devilish challenges of the school year. But it was actually born on a book tour for our first cookbook, *How to Feed a Family*. During trips to multiple cities, interviews with journalists (often parents, too), radio call-in shows and book signings, we talked to a lot of parents. And while the reaction we received to *How to Feed a Family* was enthusiastic, conversations about food and family usually ended up in the same place: "But . . . how?!" Parents in that school phase, in particular, were stressed about the volume of food that has to be shopped for, made, packed up, served, hopefully eaten, and cleaned up. And as kids get older and busier with activities, things just get tougher.

It's a landscape we know very well. Now that all of our kids are in school, we're living there, too. How do you get breakfast into kids, make it to early morning cross-country practice with a lunch packed and some snacks for the tiny window between school and ballet class? Oh, and then get everybody home for dinner and homework? Even worse, some families' schedules dictate dinner on-the-go, so meals for an entire day need to be ready to roll the day before. Add working parents, with their own hectic schedules, to the mix, and it's rough.

We started to feel like a cookbook that speaks to parents of school-aged kids has to be as much about the *how* as the *what*, when it comes to food. We wanted to answer the questions of how to get organized, create a plan and how to get the most out of your time in the kitchen. And when we floated the idea of a school year cookbook that would take it all on, the reaction from friends and strangers alike was always the same: "I need that book right now."

And so, friends, here it is. Alongside our hard-working recipes you'll find the strategies we know you'll need to pull off the school year without losing your mind. We've road-tested every bit of this book, from setting up an efficient pantry, to creating fast and delicious dishes you can cook ahead for the week, and it all absolutely makes a difference to sanity levels. Otherwise, we wouldn't have been here to write it. In our experience, using all of these strategies in concert gives the best results; however, even meal planning and baking a batch of muffins on the weekend will make a big difference to your stress levels.

As you're using this handbook for survival—we're hoping it will be dog-eared and sauce-splattered soon!— there are a few things we invite you to keep in mind.

GET ORGANIZED. There are lots of tips in the book about how to tackle food, but the bottom line is leaving as little to chance as possible. Like planning your annual Thanksgiving dinner, thinking and preparing as much in advance is the best defense against the hurricane of responsibilities that is your weekly life. Initially, it will feel hard, like more work than less. But you got this! Just like you learned to nail bedtime, this will all become routine. And you'll find the shortcuts (thank you, pre-made mixes from heaven) to make it run like clockwork. If you've never tried meal planning, expect to become evangelical after the first couple of weeks. You'll save time, money and stress.

NUTRITION COUNTS. We've not only thought about what to give your family, but in what amounts, why and when. As parents we all worry (some of us obsess) about our children's nutrition. It's why we've woven nutritional information throughout the book. However, it's not just "eat carrots for vitamin A"; we give you the tools to help you pack the most nutrition into all of your meals. From breakfasts that fire the brain for learning to lunches that hold off the 2:00 p.m. slump, we worked with a dietician to make sure the meals we're making not only feed a family but fuel them. So let go of your worry and just refer to our guides to help stack your meals with nutrition. Also, check out our section for active kids—we know there are a lot of families that cope with the challenge of children who barely have time for a meal between intense practices and games.

HOW THE RECIPES WORK. We wanted to make our recipes as easy as possible for you to use. So, of course we've highlighted those that are vegetarian, fast, portable and great for your active kids. In addition, we put a spotlight on which ones can be made ahead and stored in the freezer. But we also took a whole new approach to writing our recipes by creating and incorporating the Get Ahead stage. In this page note, we pull out the step or steps in the recipe you can do in advance. Then, when you go to prepare the dish, this important feature reduces the recipe's total time, helping you get dinner on the table quicker and easier. We thoroughly understand that there are days when the dividing line between peace and chaos can come down to a precious 15-minute window. And, like we said, your absolute best defense for a busy week is identifying where you can get ahead, so we wanted to do some of that work for you.

BOOK-EXCLUSIVE VIDEO SERIES. Throughout the book be sure to look for a screen symbol on recipes and features. We've made an exclusive series of videos that work in tandem with this book delivering even more service on mastering certain recipes or meal ideas (smoothies and grain bowls), time-saving strategies, simple how-tos (spatchcock a chicken for quicker cooking) or conquering the reinvention of leftovers. You can find them on sweetpotatochronicles.com or on the Sweet Potato Chronicles YouTube channel. You won't want to miss them.

THINK OUTSIDE THE SANDWICH. We love sandwiches as much as the next person, and include a couple recipes in the pages of this book, but in terms of making a difference in your lunch-box-packing life, we want you to consider other options. Getting out of the sandwich rut can be a game-changer for kids and parents alike for the way that it opens up a world of possibilities. And that's why . . .

WE HEART LEFTOVERS. You'll notice that our lunch chapter is one of the slimmest. It's not because we don't understand the soul-crushing nature of school lunches. In fact, it's quite the opposite. We are acutely aware that it's one of the biggest obstacles parents face in the school year; not only what to make but how to keep it healthy and appealing. That's why we created *all* of our dinner recipes with the notion that leftovers from those meals make their way into a lunch box the following day. Most of the recipes in the dinner chapter are portable and can be easily reheated or eaten cold. So when you're looking for lunch inspiration, be sure to hit the dinner chapter as well—you'll get two meals out of it, helping make sure you optimize your time in the kitchen.

But we also took leftovers head-on. That's right, no more pretending we don't see the dish of last night's chicken stuffed into the corner of the refrigerator where good food typically goes to die. We're embracing the leftover. So, we created a whole feature devoted to helping you reverse the notion that if it's a leftover then it can only be reheated. We have four brilliant recipes that repurpose a previous meal's excess, giving them a whole new look and name. It's a familiar little title that maybe you've heard of? It's called dinner. Yup, that's right, your family won't recognize those pesky leftovers and, because the recipes are comforting and classic, we're putting our money on the fact they'll eat it. Insert maniacal little laugh here.

YOU'RE NOT ALONE. Even the most enthusiastic home cook can be brought low by the grind of the school year. Don't even believe for a second that we gleefully skip into the kitchen every day! But a key to not feeling like the family short order cook is to stop acting like it. Get the whole family to buy in to the weekly meal plan and give everyone some responsibility. Older kids can help with prep or prepare simple meals or dishes, younger kids can set the table, and whatever they're doing, the more involved they are, the better. Kids who are part of food prep (in whatever way that works for you) are more likely to eat the food. You're also teaching them important life skills and, well, it's fair.

THERE'S NO FAILING GRADE. Lucky for us, the school year is broken into bite-sized pieces called days, weeks and months. And when you have a week that falls apart, there's always another waiting around the corner. This book is designed to be a touchstone; a place where you can go back to, again and again, to find information and inspiration to help you get back on track. Lord knows, we need it too.

By the time children make it to school age, the one thing that every single parent since the dawn of civilization has marveled at is how incredibly fast time passes. So because the pause button on childhood is as elusive as the fountain of youth, it is our sincere wish that the outcome of all our research, strategies, time-saving recipes and shortcuts in *The School Year Survival Cookbook* give you the one thing we all want and need more of: time with our family. So go ahead and enjoy the view and, of course, the meal.

A PANTRY FOR SUCCESS

Nothing takes the pressure off meal prep more than knowing your pantry has your back. And in the long-distance race that is the school year, every advantage is worth taking. You don't need an enormous pantry to support your cooking efforts—you just need the one that works for your family and what you like to eat. And by "pantry" we mean your cupboards, freezer and fridge—anywhere you keep basics. We're going to, ahem, assume you're cooking from the recipes in this book, so our recommendations for pantry items reflect our meals. Having the items you need over and over again organized and at arm's length is a bit like having an in-house sous-chef. But one that you created. Because you're so amazing. **LK**

HOW TO BEGIN

1 PURGE YOUR CUPBOARDS. Start not by filling your cupboards, but by emptying them. Do this in August, before your kids head back to school and your schedule goes haywire. You wouldn't send the kids to school without backpacks, so don't even think about taking on September unless you've set yourself up to succeed. A rainy Saturday (or two) gets this job done.

2 DO AN EDIT. Take everything out of your cabinets and place it all on your counters, kitchen table or even the floor.

3 CLEANING COUNTS. Give every shelf, rack and drawer a wipe-down with warm, soapy water. Critters—and not the cute ones known as your children—love pantries, sadly, and regular cleaning is the only way to keep them out.

4 TIME TO TOSS. Bin things that (a) you don't use regularly, (b) are older than a year or (c) you don't recognize. Be honest with yourself. Is this really the year you're going to start using that lavender-scented honey in your tea? If not, au revoir, honey! The space you're creating by tossing out the bulk cereal that no one really liked is going to make room for fresh ingredients that will make your meals taste better.

SETUP FOR SUCCESS

5 CREATE A SYSTEM. It's important to organize your space in a way that makes sense for how you work in the kitchen. The most basic step toward this is being able to see your ingredients clearly.

6 GLASS CONTAINERS FOR DRY GOODS. We recommend storing flours, sugars, grains and nuts in an assortment of glass containers in large, medium and small sizes. Glass is best for food safety and won't absorb odors or colors the way plastics can. Use traditional canning jars or recycled jam jars, or pick up plain screw-top glass jars at a home store. Before using, run everything—jars and lids both—through the sterilize setting of the dishwasher. Dry them well, then fill them up. Clip any cooking instructions you'll need in the future or product descriptions (Lord knows, it's hard to tell wheat flour from spelt flour) and tape them to the container for easy reference. If you're like Ceri, go ahead and toss the instructions right in the jar. Now you can see each item, know how much is left, stack them if you need to, and have fewer spills when you open the cupboard door.

7 PUT WATERPROOF LABELS ON CONTAINERS. You don't want to make a tragic salt-for-sugar mistake, so label everything clearly, using waterproof labels and permanent ink. The kitchen is a sticky place, so those labels need to survive the dishwasher.

8 **MAKE STAPLE ITEMS EASY TO REACH.** If you use it daily, place it in the most accessible spot in your cupboard. Where possible, particularly on upper shelves, try not to have too many multiple rows in cupboards.

9 **ORGANIZE FOODS IN LIKE GROUPINGS.** For instance, cluster all your flours together, and the same with sugars, cans of beans and soups, and containers of grains (like rice, cereal, pastas and cornmeal).

10 **STORE SPICES IN A CUPBOARD.** You may love the look of spices in a rack up on the wall, but it's not the best way to prolong their freshness. Keep spices in a cool, dark spot, like a cupboard or a drawer, and in airtight containers to keep them fresh longer. Check to see if your spices are still viable by giving them a sniff. No scent? No good! Buy spices in small quantities, as they won't stay fresh and flavorful for longer than a year.

11 **KEEP OILS AND VINEGARS AWAY FROM LIGHT AND HEAT.** But store them close to your workspace. Most oils and vinegars have a two-year shelf life unopened. If you've cracked the cap, you generally have 3 to 6 months to use them. Store cooking sprays alongside your oils as well.

12 **SALT AND PEPPER ARE ESSENTIAL FOR COOKING.** Given how frequently you'll be reaching for them, keep salt and pepper in your kitchen's prime reach-for-it spot.

13 **DON'T BUY IN BULK—UNLESS YOU'RE GOING TO WHIZ THROUGH THE WHOLE SHEBANG IN A WEEK.** Buying a bag of almonds that weighs as much as a toddler might seem like great value, but remember you'll need to store them and eat them before they expire.

14 **FIRST IN, FIRST OUT.** If you have multiples of ingredients, be sure to pull the oldest ones to the front of the fridge or cupboard and line up the newest ones at the back.

15 **MAINTAIN THE SYSTEM.** Empty dry pantry items into your jars, fresh herbs into jars in the refrigerator, and oils into their containers (if it's your preference, and if you're like us, because your easy-reach spot is out on the counter) as soon as you're back from the grocery store each week.

PANTRY PREFERENCES

We know we sound a bit bossy-pants with all this pantry business, but it's all meant to make your life easier once the school year hits. So here's the final word on a few things: Our recipes are designed to be flexible and will not fall apart if you don't have the same brand of butter that we used in our recipe testing. However, we do have some preferences.

MILK: Unless we specify otherwise, we're assuming you're using cow's milk (any percent). But if your family prefers non-dairy options such as coconut, almond, cashew or soy, go ahead. Laura is a big fan of coconut milk but switches to cow's milk when she thinks the coconut flavor won't complement what she's making. We don't love the taste of almond milk in something like a frittata, but if it doesn't bother you, go for it.

BUTTER: We always use unsalted butter, but if you prefer salted, you're likely accustomed to reducing accordingly the salt amount the recipes call for, or are satisfied by the flavor the additional salt gives the dish.

OATS: We prefer whole rolled oats or steel-cut oats rather than quick-cooking oats. They take a bit longer to cook but deliver better health benefits.

GREASING: We like to use plain old butter or coconut oil spray to grease our baking pans. If you like nonstick sprays or other oils, feel free to use them.

(Glad we had this talk.)

THE **SWEET POTATO CHRONICLES PANTRY**

CUPBOARDS

The majority of your pantry lives here, so keep them clean and well stocked.

OILS AND VINEGARS
Olive oil (extra-virgin is worth the expense for dressings and drizzling, but virgin is fine for cooking)
Neutral-flavored oil such as grapeseed or vegetable
Sesame oil
Coconut oil
Cooking spray
Plain vinegar (good for cleaning, too!)
White wine and red wine vinegar
Rice wine vinegar (not "seasoned")
Apple cider vinegar
Balsamic vinegar

FLOURS
All-purpose flour
Corn flour
Gluten-free flours (if your home requires them)
Spelt flour
Whole wheat flour

SUGARS AND SYRUPS
Agave nectar
Brown rice syrup or corn syrup
Brown sugar
Cane sugar
Confectioners' sugar
Honey
Maple syrup

GRAINS AND PASTA
Breadcrumbs: plain, panko
Grains: cornmeal/polenta, pearl barley, quinoa
Granola
Lentils: brown, red
Muesli
Oats: rolled, steel-cut

Pasta: standard, whole grain, rice, couscous
Rice: basmati, brown, jasmine
Seeds: chia, raw shelled hemp, pumpkin, sunflower

CANNED/BOXED GOODS
Beans: black, cannellini, chickpeas, red kidney
Coconut milk: full-fat or light
Pumpkin purée
Tomatoes: whole, diced, paste, sun-dried
Tuna (packed in oil)

DRIED HERBS AND SPICES
Bay leaves
Chili powder
Curry powder
Dry mustard
Garam masala
Garlic powder
Ground allspice
Ground cardamom
Ground cinnamon
Ground cloves
Ground coriander
Ground cumin
Ground ginger
Ground turmeric
Dried oregano
Whole nutmeg

BAKING SUPPLIES
Almond extract
Baking powder
Baking soda
Chocolate: baking, chips
Cornstarch
Dried fruits: apricots, blueberries, cranberries, goji berries, raisins, banana chips
Cocoa powder (Dutch-process)
Unsweetened shredded coconut

OTHERS

Almond butter
Non-nut butter such as sunflower butter
Popping corn
Tahini
Umami paste
Garlic
Onions
Potatoes: new, sweet, white

FRIDGE

What fills your fridge will change week to week with your meal plans, but here are some items you'll always want handy.

BASICS

Applesauce
Milk: cow's, almond, coconut
Butter (unsalted)
Eggs
Yogurt: plain Greek-style
Ground flax
Fresh ginger
Citrus: lemons, limes

CONDIMENTS AND SAUCES

Jams
Mustard: Dijon or whole grain
Hot sauce: Tabasco, Sriracha
Mayonnaise or Vegenaise
Ketchup (come on, you know they're going to ask)
Worcestershire sauce
Soy sauce

FREEZER

The final frontier of your pantry is for far more than just ice cream. The freezer is the ultimate out-of-sight, out-of-mind zone, so be sure to label and date everything. The quality of frozen food (texture, flavor, nutrients) declines over time, so keep frozen fruits and veg for 8 to 12 months tops, pre-cooked foods for 2 to 3 months, and most other items for 3 to 6 months. To maintain freshness, seal out air and moisture by using resealable freezer bags and glass or plastic containers designed for the freezer.

FREEZER ESSENTIALS

Bacon
Bread
Chicken: skinless, boneless breasts and thighs
Dough: pizza, phyllo
Ground meat: beef, turkey
Fruit: berries, bananas, peaches, mangoes
Nuts: almonds, macadamias, walnuts or pecans
Vegetables: corn, peas, chopped spinach, chopped kale

THE MIXES

These easy-to-assemble mixes will bail you out time and time again. If you keep them in your pantry, you're always only a scoop away from brilliance, from breakfast staples to favorite snacks. These can live in your pantry for months in an airtight container.

WHOLE GRAIN PANCAKE AND WAFFLE MIX

Makes: enough for 4 batches

6 cups (1.5 L)	spelt flour
1 Tbsp (15 ml)	salt
1 Tbsp (15 ml)	baking powder
1 tsp (5 ml)	baking soda

(1) In a large bowl, sift together the spelt flour, salt, baking powder and baking soda. Store in an airtight container in a cool, dry spot and use within 6 months.

PANCAKES

Makes: 6 to 8 pancakes

2 cups (500 ml)	Whole Grain Pancake and Waffle Mix
2 tsp (10 ml)	ground cinnamon
1	large egg
1¾ cups (425 ml)	milk
1 Tbsp (15 ml)	maple syrup
½ tsp (2 ml)	vanilla extract

(1) In a large bowl, whisk together the dry mix and cinnamon. In a medium bowl, whisk together the egg, milk, maple syrup and vanilla. Pour the wet ingredients into the dry ingredients and stir until just combined. Let rest for 10 minutes.

(2) While the batter rests, heat a griddle or large nonstick pan over medium heat. Once hot, coat griddle or pan with nonstick spray (or use butter plus a little vegetable oil to keep the butter from burning). Pour about ¼ cup (60 ml) of batter onto the hot griddle for each pancake. Once large bubbles pop to the surface, after 2 to 3 minutes, flip and cook another 2 minutes. Repeat with remaining batter.

WAFFLES

Makes: about 3 large waffles

1½ cup (375 ml)	Whole Grain Pancake and Waffle Mix
¾ cup (175 ml)	milk
½ cup (125 ml)	buttermilk
2	eggs, lightly beaten
2 Tbsp (30 ml)	oil

(1) Preheat your waffle iron.

(2) Place the dry mix in a large bowl. Add the milk, buttermilk, eggs and oil and stir until just combined. Let rest for 10 minutes.

(3) Coat waffle iron with oil or nonstick spray. Follow the waffle iron's instructions for cooking, greasing the iron in between batches if needed.

MULTIGRAIN MUFFIN MIX
Makes: enough for 4 dozen muffins

6 cups (1.5 L)	whole wheat flour
1 cup (250 ml)	oats
1 cup (250 ml)	ground flax
1 cup (250 ml)	raw shelled hemp seeds
½ cup (125 ml)	chia seeds
4 Tbsp (60 ml)	baking powder
4 tsp (20 ml)	baking soda
2 tsp (10 ml)	salt

1. In a large bowl, whisk together the flour, oats, ground flax, hemp seeds, chia seeds, baking powder, baking soda and salt. Store in an airtight container in a cool, dry spot and use within 6 months.

MUFFINS
Makes: 1 dozen muffins

2	eggs
1 cup (250 ml)	yogurt
⅓ cup (75 ml)	vegetable oil
½ cup (125 ml)	sugar
1 tsp (5 ml)	vanilla extract
2 cups (500 ml)	Multigrain Muffin Mix
¾ cup (175 ml)	optional extras: blueberries, sliced apple, pecans, chocolate chips

1. Preheat the oven to 350°F (180°C). Line a 12-cup muffin tin with paper liners and give them a light spray of oil.

2. In a large bowl, whisk together the eggs, yogurt, oil, sugar and vanilla until combined. Shake the muffin mix over the wet mixture and stir until just combined. Don't overmix the batter or you'll have tough muffins! Gently fold in any extras you're adding.

3. Spoon the batter into muffin liners. Bake for 18 to 20 minutes, until a toothpick inserted in the center comes out clean. Tip baked muffins onto a rack to cool.

BASIC BUTTERY BISCUIT MIX
Makes: enough for about 20 biscuits

3 cups (750 ml)	spelt flour
2 cups (500 ml)	all-purpose flour
4 tsp (20 ml)	baking powder
1 tsp (5 ml)	baking soda
1 tsp (5 ml)	salt

1. In a large bowl, sift together the spelt flour, all-purpose flour, baking powder, baking soda and salt. Store in an airtight container in a cool, dry spot and use within 6 months.

BISCUITS
Makes: about 10 biscuits

2½ cups (625 ml)	Basic Buttery Biscuit Mix
½ cup (125 ml)	cold butter, cut into chunks
¾ cup (175 ml)	milk
1 Tbsp (15 ml)	maple syrup or fresh herbs
2	eggs, beaten and divided
½ cup (125 ml)	optional extra: cheddar cheese, grated

1. Preheat the oven to 400°F (200°C). Line a baking sheet with parchment paper.

2. Place the biscuit mix and butter in a food processor. Process until mixture resembles a coarse crumb. Pour into a large bowl.

3. Using a fork, stir in the milk, maple syrup and 1 egg until the dough just comes together.

4. Turn out dough onto a lightly floured surface and gently knead it only about three times, then pat out into a disk ½ inch (1 cm) thick. Cut out biscuits using a lightly floured biscuit cutter or glass; cut about 10, re-rolling any scraps. Place them on the baking sheet. Brush the tops with 1 beaten egg.

5. Bake for 10 to 12 minutes, until lightly browned and a toothpick inserted in the center comes out clean. Serve warm with butter and jam.

GEARING UP

The kitchen gear you're going to need for the school year is almost as important as the food. These kitchen components are essential to cooking along with this book and will make your life easier in general.

FOR THE FAMILY MEALS, you'll want to suit up your kitchen with some specific appliances, including a slow cooker, food processor and blender. You'll also need plenty of food storage bags (in various sizes) and food storage containers (in either plastic or glass, although glass is best for reheating right in the container).

FOR SCHOOL LUNCHES, if your children are between four and ten, then bento-style lunch boxes will likely better suit your little grazer. Their multiple compartments mean you're able to offer the variety that younger children respond to and enjoy. For older children, choose large containers that can accommodate bigger portions of single dishes they will like to see in their lunches, like salads or pastas.

A WATER BOTTLE should suit your child's age and be BPA-free. For instance, younger children will do best with a bottle that has a pull spout, whereas older kids can manage twisting off a screw top to drink from the container without spilling the contents across their desk.

It's also important to have the following to guarantee food safety:

A THERMAL LUNCH CARRY CASE: You'll want to make sure this case has enough room for your containers and allows them to be stored upright to guard against spills. Many cases come with their own storage containers designed to fit snugly in the bags.

A THERMOS: You'll need one for hot meals like soups and chilies. Preheat the thermos by filling with hot water for a few minutes, then empty and fill with hot food.

GEL-FREE ICE PACKS: Look for packs filled with purified water. Gel explosions can be messy and contaminate the food.

THE RIGHT GEAR FOR THE KID: If you're sending your child off to school for the first time (you're going to be fine), have them try opening and closing everything on their own in advance. You can't count on teachers or lunch supervisors to have time to help out every kid. (Seriously, you're going to be fine!)

THIS IS DINNER

MON: SUNDRIED TOMATO
& SPINACH PENNE

TUES: HALIBUT TACOS

WED: BUTTER CHICKEN

THURS: BUTTER CHICKEN
GRAIN BOWL

FRI: SUNDRIED TOMATO
& SPINACH PESTO
PIZZA

MEAL PLANNING FOR SANITY

Everything you've heard about meal planning is true. It's wildly un-sexy. And it will change your life in every imaginable way—seriously! Knowing what you're going to buy, what you're going to cook and when you're going to eat those meals will save you time, money and stress. Of these three, the most important saving is to your sanity. When we talk with parents about the challenges of feeding a family, the dilemma of what to make each night (and morning and midday) tops the charts. Although tossing out those desiccated carrots you never got around to using is quite a heartbreaker, too.

There are a few different ways to create a meal plan, and we're sharing what we think works best for most families. Yes, there are people out there planning their menus monthly and even quarterly, but given that most of us grocery shop weekly, we've landed on the week as our perfect time unit. **CM**

HERE'S HOW WE BREAK IT DOWN

1 KNOW EVERYONE'S SCHEDULE. And we mean *everyone*. Meal planning only works when you factor in what everyone is doing each day. Draw up a family calendar, where you can list all lessons, practices, tutor sessions, later-than-usual meetings and anything else that might alter the basic flow of your days. Whether your calendar is tacked to the fridge or you have another hub for family information, be sure it's in a place where you and everyone else can check back to it, and kids can be sent when they ask, "What's for supper?"

2 MAKE A RECIPE LIST. List all the recipes you want to eat during the week, including breakfasts, lunches, snacks, dinners and sides. We recommend having this discussion sometime when the whole family can be together and look at the week ahead—say, Friday dinner or Saturday brunch. Have everyone in your family make suggestions—and take into consideration the events on the calendar you created. For instance, if one of your kids is coming home late from back-to-back hockey practices on Tuesday nights, that's not your day for introducing a new or challenging ingredient. Instead, you want to be rustling up his favorite pasta recipe. Think about which recipes will yield leftovers for the next day's lunches (we've included lots of those in our dinner chapter). Plan at least one vegetarian day, and generally keep a range of nutritional highlights in mind over the course of your weekly plan. Don't forget sides—you may not need recipes for every side dish, but include them in your list. And there's no need to toss out those family traditions. If Tuesdays are taco nights or Fridays are when you all go out for sushi, you can easily tick off an evening's dinner plan.

3 CREATE YOUR PLAN. With your schedule and recipe list complete, you're ready to put them together. Think of using up your produce early in the week and leaning on your pantry later in the week. You might want to work on a piece of paper before committing everything to the calendar.

4 **MAKE A GROCERY LIST.** Oh, not so fast! Make that list standing in your kitchen. As you come to each recipe on your plan, quickly check to see if you've already got what you need in the fridge, freezer or cupboards. The week you skip this step will be the time you learn you're panko millionaires. For maximum efficiency, organize your list in the order that reflects your path through the grocery store or market. Hit the store with your list in hand. If you go rogue, it will be because the local corn is too beautiful to leave behind, not because you're grabbing for random vegetables without a plan for cooking them.

5 **PUT IT AWAY.** Arrive home with your groceries (and a good feeling in your heart). All pantry items should come out of their boxes, bags and wrappings and be put away in the appropriate pantry container (check out our pantry how-to on pp. 5-6).

6 **YAY, YOU!** Congratulate yourself on creating a meal plan, which is to say, doing half of the heavy lifting involved in getting everyone fed for another week. You are a hero.

TIP See our recipe for Sweet Potato Chips with Yogurt Dipping Sauce on page 190.

MEAL PLAN

Here's how a meal plan would work in real life. For this example we'll use a week in the middle of winter, with the following particulars: Two kids taking packed lunches to school every day except Tuesday, which is pizza day. Swimming lessons on Monday evening and dance after school on Thursday. Mom has a late meeting on Wednesday night and Dad has soccer on Thursdays.

SATURDAY PREP FOR THE WEEK

AM: With your grocery list in hand, hit the market.
PM: Make Coconut Lentil Soup and Beet Hummus and store them in the fridge for the week.

SUNDAY PREP FOR THE WEEK

PM: Make a batch each of both Carrot Cake Breakfast Cookies and Broccoli and Cheese Patties and get them in the freezer (minus the four patties that are going in tomorrow's lunch). Involve the kids in making School-Safe Chocolate Snack Balls. Pack lunches. Before going to bed, toss the ingredients for the Peanut Butter and Banana Sandwich Slow Cooker Oats into the machine and turn it on—it will make enough for 2 days.

	MONDAY	TUESDAY
BREAKFAST	Peanut Butter and Banana Sandwich Slow Cooker Oats (page 39)	Peanut Butter and Banana Sandwich Slow Cooker Oats (page 39)
LUNCH	Broccoli and Cheese Patties with cucumber, carrots and grapes (page 80)	Red peppers and blueberries for pizza day
SNACKS	School-Safe Chocolate Snack Balls and blueberries (page 170)	Carrot Cake Breakfast Cookies (page 28)
DINNER	Coconut Lentil Soup with green salad (page 73)	Turkey Meatloaf with Apples and Sage, mashed potatoes and green beans (page 139)
EVENING PREP FOR TOMORROW	Don't forget it's pizza day at school tomorrow! Prep and pack blueberries and red peppers for school snack. Chop and combine ingredients for Tuesday's meatloaf so those babies get in the oven quicker.	Make meatloaf sammies for lunches and chop veggies for after-school snack and dinner frittata.

Everything you've heard about meal planning is true. It's wildly unsexy. And it will change your life.

WEDNESDAY	THURSDAY	FRIDAY
Cinnamon raisin toast with peanut butter, banana, coconut and nutmeg *(page 43)*	Chocolate Avocado Chia Pudding with berries *(page 41)*	Carrot Cake Breakfast Cookies with yogurt and fruit *(page 28)*
Meatloaf sammie with red peppers and grapes *(page 139)*	Leftover frittata with carrots and mango	Chickpea and Cauliflower Curry with Brown Rice, with cucumber, cherry tomatoes and grapes *(page 152)*
Beet Hummus with carrots *(page 184)*	School-Safe Chocolate Snack Balls *(page 170)*	Beet Hummus with veggies *(page 184)*
Kale, Sweet Potato and Goat Cheese Frittata with green beans *(page 96)*	Chickpea and Cauliflower Curry with Brown Rice *(page 152)*	Baked Fried Chicken with egg noodles and broccoli *(page 141)*
Dice veggies for curry and pack leftover frittata for lunches. Stir together Chia Pudding ingredients and place in fridge.	Take chicken out of the freezer and place in the fridge so it's ready to go when you get home. Pack leftover curry into lunches and chop veggies for lunch and after-school snack.	

"I actually don't really feel like eating breakfast most school mornings but I can never say no to my mom's overnight oats."

SCARLETT, AGE 10

"Breakfast is my favorite meal.

"Ooh, breakfast. I'd like pancakes with whip cream and M&Ms and every candy in the world. I've never had that but I'm sure it's good."

ESME, AGE 10

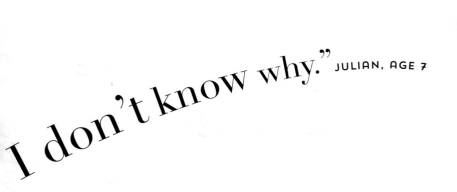

I don't know why." JULIAN, AGE 7

Breakfast

E- Good luc
your report +
you'll be g

Love,
Mum.
P.S. Ple

MAKE A BRAINY BREAKFAST

A s a parent, there's a lot of pressure on you when it comes to choosing the programs your child should be in to get to the head of the class. From early-reader groups to after-school mathlete classes, parents aren't short on choices for extracurriculars meant to help boost academic success. But there's one program every parent should sign up for—it's the best one out there, free, and, guess what, it doesn't have a waiting list: healthy nutrition. Studies have shown that certain foods, in the right combinations, can boost brain function, enhance memory and improve concentration. That's why it's so important for school-age children to start their day with a well-rounded breakfast. In fact, research has shown breakfast skippers have more trouble academically and can be prone to behavioral issues.

The best way to set your children up for a timetable that includes a rigorous period of multiplication, quiet reading time (please sit still!) and an energetic game of four square is to provide them with a breakfast that delivers the right amount of brain fuel. Carbohydrates are the gas the brain needs, but you need to choose the right kinds. Aim for whole grains such as oatmeal rather than refined or sugary carbs like donuts or toaster pastries. A breakfast laden with sugar gives a quick burst of energy followed by hunger. But whole grain carbs (with fiber) provide long-lasting energy. **LK**

BALANCE BLOOD SUGAR. Pick carbohydrates that have slow-releasing sugars to keep kids fired and ready for learning all morning. Try foods like oatmeal, quinoa and bread made from whole grain wheat or whole rye.

PAIR PROTEIN WITH CARBS. Proteins throw on the brakes when it comes to absorbing sugars found in carbs, so add nuts, nut butters and plain or Greek-style yogurt to the morning meal of, let's say, oats. Another great source of protein is eggs. The choline found in the whites helps with memory development, so there's even more reason to put an egg on it.

ADD ANTIOXIDANTS. There's a reason there's so much chatter about antioxidants: not only can they prevent cell damage but they can help halt it, too. These nutrients also further fuel the brain to help with learning, so add to the mix foods like blueberries, strawberries, blackberries and cherries—the more intense the color, the bigger the nutritional punch.

BLUEBERRY PIE FRENCH TOAST MUFFINS

We're longtime French toast fans in our home, so when my daughter, Scarlett, started school I tried to maintain the routine by making the French toast in the evening and then reheating the slices in the morning. Eventually, I created these muffins—using the flavors in my favorite blueberry pie recipe—as a more efficient way to keep my girl's beloved morning meal on rotation. **LK**

MAKES **8** *Muffins*	PREP TIME **10** *Minutes*	TOTAL TIME **25** *Minutes*	PORTABLE, MAKE AHEAD, VEGETARIAN

8	eggs
¾ cup (175 ml)	milk
1 tsp (5 ml)	vanilla extract
¼ tsp (1 ml)	lemon zest
½ tsp (2 ml)	lemon juice
¼ tsp (1 ml)	ground allspice
¼ tsp (1 ml)	salt
8	thick slices of whole grain bread, cut into cubes
¼ cup (60 ml)	blueberries

1. Preheat the oven to 350°F (180°C). Grease 8 cups of a 12-cup muffin tin.

2. In a large bowl, whisk together the eggs, milk, vanilla, lemon zest, lemon juice, allspice and salt. Add the bread cubes and stir, making sure all the cubes are covered in eggy mixture. Let soak for 5 minutes.

3. Fold in the blueberries. Spoon the bread mixture into muffin cups. Bake for 12 to 14 minutes, until the egg is cooked and the muffins are golden brown. Turn out onto a rack to cool completely. Store in an airtight container in the refrigerator for up to 1 week.

TIP This recipe lends itself to any seasonal fruit. To reheat these babies, pop them into the toaster oven with the rack on the lowest level and heat them for 4 to 6 minutes. Serve with a drizzle of maple syrup or honey. If you're eating on the go, use a healthy smear of jam to avoid a sticky mess.

YOGURT PARFAIT POPSICLES

These creamy popsicles are really just a delivery system for fruit and anything else you feel like shoehorning inside. I felt a little flax oil wouldn't hurt, so there you have it—an easy way to add omega-3. Besides, "Grab your socks and eat your popsicle!" is like music to a kid's ears in the morning. It's almost as good as hearing, "There's no school today!" Almost, but not quite. **LK**

MAKES 10 *Popsicles*	**PREP TIME** 20 *Minutes*	**TOTAL TIME** 3 *Hours* 20 *Minutes*

PORTABLE, MAKE AHEAD, VEGETARIAN

2½ cups (625 ml)   plain Greek-style yogurt
1 cup (250 ml)   milk
3 Tbsp (45 ml)   honey, plus more for drizzle
1 tsp (5 ml)   flax oil
2 Tbsp (30 ml)   granola

FRUIT FILLING—USE ANY COMBO OF THE FOLLOWING:
½   banana, sliced
handful of   blueberries
handful of   raspberries
handful of   sliced kiwi

1. In a medium bowl, stir together yogurt, milk, honey and flax oil.

2. Arrange half the fruit pieces in the bottom of popsicle molds. Pour in enough yogurt mixture to fill each mold halfway. Tap mold on the counter to remove any air bubbles that will be the death of your pops after they're frozen.

3. Drop in the remaining fruit pieces. Tap mold again to settle everything.

4. Fill each mold almost to the top with the remaining yogurt mix, leaving just enough space for the granola. Tap mold again. Drizzle honey onto the yogurt to act as "glue," then sprinkle with granola. Gently insert popsicle sticks, then give it all a final tap. Freeze for at least 3 hours.

TIP The yogurt mix in these guys
is the perfect canvas for any
seasonal fruits your family enjoys.

CARROT CAKE BREAKFAST COOKIES

The hint of cinnamon combined with the carrots and the slight rise of these cookies really does give them a carrot cake feeling. But make no mistake, these are hard-working breakfast bites that are packed with veggies and fiber. You can add them to a sit-down breakfast with yogurt and fruit or eat them on the run. Days that start with cookies are just bound to be the best. **CM**

MAKES **40** *Small Cookies* | **PREP TIME** **40** *Minutes* | **TOTAL TIME** **55** *Minutes*

VEGETARIAN, MAKE AHEAD, PORTABLE

1 cup (250 ml)	oats
¾ cup (175 ml)	whole wheat flour
1½ tsp (7 ml)	baking powder
1 tsp (5 ml)	ground cinnamon
¼ tsp (1 ml)	salt
1	egg
1 tsp (5 ml)	vanilla extract
½ cup (125 ml)	maple syrup
2 Tbsp (30 ml)	coconut oil or butter, melted
¾ cup (175 ml)	grated carrots (2 medium carrots)

1. Preheat the oven to 350°F (180°C). Line two baking sheets with parchment paper.

2. In a medium bowl, stir together the oats, flour, baking powder, cinnamon and salt. In a large bowl, whisk together the egg, vanilla, maple syrup and coconut oil. Add the dry ingredients to the wet ones and stir until just combined. Now stir in your carrots.

3. If you have time, chill your dough for about half an hour. This will stop the cookies from spreading out too much in the oven. If you don't have time, not to worry, you'll have thinner but still delicious cookies.

4. Drop tablespoon-sized balls of dough onto the baking sheets, leaving an inch or two (2.5 to 5 cm) between each. Bake for 12 to 15 minutes in the middle rack, until cookies are brown at the edges and just set on top. Let cool for a few minutes before transferring to a rack to cool completely. They'll keep in an airtight container for up to 5 days or freeze for up to a month.

BAKED APPLE CINNAMON OATMEAL

You could make this entire recipe on the morning you intend to eat it, but you'd have to get up pretty early, and I believe we're all getting up plenty early as it is, right? So I mix up my ingredients in a cake pan the night before, then put it in the oven when I get up and let the intoxicatingly sweet smell of hot, cinnamony appleness wake my kids. I love the feeling of giving everyone a hot breakfast on a chilly morning. I also love knowing that this recipe feeds a family of four two days running. **CM**

MAKES **8** *Servings*	PREP TIME **10** *Minutes*	TOTAL TIME **50** *Minutes*	VEGETARIAN, MAKE AHEAD

2 cups (500 ml)	oats
1/3 cup (75 ml)	brown sugar
1 tsp (5 ml)	baking powder
1 tsp (5 ml)	ground cinnamon
1/2 tsp (2 ml)	salt
1	egg
2 cups (500 ml)	milk
1 cup (250 ml)	applesauce
3 Tbsp (45 ml)	butter, melted
1 1/2 tsp (7 ml)	vanilla extract
1 1/2 cups (375 ml)	chopped unpeeled apple (firm apples like Gala or Honeycrisp work well)
1/2 cup (125 ml)	chopped almonds, pecans or walnuts (optional)

1. Preheat the oven to 350°F (180°C). Lightly grease an 8-inch (20 cm) square cake pan.

2. In a large bowl, stir together oats, sugar, baking powder, cinnamon and salt. In a medium bowl, whisk together the egg, milk, applesauce, butter and vanilla. Add the wet ingredients to the dry ones and stir until just combined. Stir in the chopped apples and the nuts (if using).

3. Pour the batter into the pan. (If you're doing this the night before, cover and refrigerate overnight.) Bake for 35 to 40 minutes, until oatmeal is firmly set. Serve warm with a drizzle of maple syrup. Cover leftovers and refrigerate. It warms up perfectly the next day.

TIP Because oats are a high-fiber, slow-burning carb, your kid will be full and fueled all morning.

BAKED OATMEAL CUPS

Necessity was absolutely the mother of this invention. When we signed up for our school's cross-country team, it meant our morning routine got even more compacted on practice days. I say "we" because Julian would only agree to join if I ran with him, so go ahead and picture me running the track with a pack of six-year-olds. So I started thinking about how our healthy and hearty standby of porridge could be quicker if it were grab-and-go. The result is these super-moist, individual, baked oatmeal cups. The nice thing is you can keep everyone's tastes in mind with the toppings and really mix them up. **CM**

MAKES **12** *Oatmeal Cups*	PREP TIME **10** *Minutes*	TOTAL TIME **40** *Minutes*	VEGETARIAN, MAKE AHEAD, PORTABLE

2	eggs
½ cup (125 ml)	brown sugar
¼ cup (60 ml)	melted coconut oil
1½ cups (375 ml)	milk
½ cup (125 ml)	applesauce (or 1 ripe banana, mashed)
2 tsp (10 ml)	vanilla extract
1 Tbsp (15 ml)	ground cinnamon
2 tsp (10 ml)	baking powder
½ tsp (2 ml)	salt
3 cups (750 ml)	oats
⅓ cup (75 ml)	ground flax
Toppings:	chopped nuts, seasonal fruits, chocolate chips or seeds

1. Preheat the oven to 350°F (180°C). Line a 12-cup muffin tin with paper liners.

2. In a large bowl, whisk together the eggs, sugar and coconut oil until well combined. Add the milk, applesauce, vanilla, cinnamon, baking powder and salt; give it a good stir. Stir in the oats and ground flax until everything is well combined.

3. Use a ¼-cup (60 ml) measure to scoop the batter into the muffin liners. Press a scattering of toppings onto each muffin. Bake for 30 minutes until oatmeal is completely set. Serve warm or at room temperature. Keep in an airtight container for 3 days or freeze for up to a month.

HUEVOS RANCHEROS BREAKFAST BURRITOS

Julian would eat a burrito for breakfast every day if I were willing to make it for him. I do make quick ones with a fried egg and grated cheese folded into a tortilla, but to be honest, it's a bit of a beige breakfast. I'd rather spend some time on the weekend setting up a little burrito factory and put together these zesty, colorful babies. They're packed with protein, iron and B-vitamins as well as vitamins A, C and E. It's a bit more effort than the quickies, but it makes enough for many healthy breakfasts, so I'm good with that. **CM**

MAKES **10** *Burritos*	PREP TIME **50** *Minutes*	TOTAL TIME **1** *Hour* **15** *Minutes*	VEGETARIAN, MAKE AHEAD

5 cups (1.25 L)	cubed peeled butternut squash (½-inch/1 cm cubes)
1 Tbsp (15 ml)	olive oil
1 tsp (5 ml)	chili powder
½ tsp (2 ml)	ground cumin
½ tsp (2 ml)	ground cinnamon
1 can (14 oz/398 ml)	black beans, drained and rinsed
6	eggs
pinch of	salt and pepper
1 Tbsp (15 ml)	butter
10	flour tortillas (10-inch/25 cm)
3 cups (750 ml)	grated cheddar cheese
1	avocado, thinly sliced
	salsa

1. Preheat the oven to 350°F (180°C).

2. Spread the cubed squash on a baking sheet. Drizzle with the oil, then sprinkle with the chili powder, cumin and cinnamon. Toss until well coated. Bake for 20 minutes.

3. Remove from the oven and add the beans to the baking sheet. Give everything a stir and spread it out evenly. Bake for another 20 minutes.

4. Meanwhile, in a large bowl, whisk the eggs with a good pinch of salt and pepper.

5. Melt the butter in a skillet over medium heat. Pour in the eggs. Stir them gently as they cook. Let them just set—don't overcook! Remove from the heat.

6. Lay out the tortillas on a work surface. Spoon about ½ cup (125 ml) of the squash and bean mixture into the middle of each tortilla in a rectangular shape, leaving a margin of tortilla on either end. Sprinkle each with about ⅓ cup (75 ml) cheese. Next, spoon over the scrambled eggs, then lay avocado slices on top. Finish off with a bit of salsa if your family likes it.

7. Working with one tortilla at a time, fold the bottom up over the filling. Pressing the joined edge down, pull back, slightly squishing the filling back toward yourself. You'll have a tube shape. Now fold in the side flaps of the tube and then roll your burrito until it is closed.

8. To freeze, wrap each burrito in plastic wrap and then foil. Label with a permanent marker with a date. Freeze for up to 1 month. Reheat in the microwave for 2 minutes or in a toaster oven set at 350°F (180°C) for 20 minutes after removing wrapping.

TIP Have your plastic wrap and foil handy when you start assembling your burritos.

PROTEIN PANCAKES WITH COTTAGE CHEESE

These pancakes are best made on the weekend and used throughout the week to power your sport-loving kids. With a cup of cottage cheese added to the batter, these flapjacks boost calcium and protein and can be eaten on the go, acting as the bread for a sandwich filled with nut butter and jam. So forget the vending machines, they don't love you like we do. **LK**

MAKES 6 *Pancakes*	**PREP TIME** 5 *Minutes*	**TOTAL TIME** 20 *Minutes*	ACTIVE KIDS, PORTABLE, MAKE AHEAD

1 cup (250 ml)	whole wheat flour
½ tsp (2 ml)	baking soda
¼ tsp (1 ml)	salt
¼ tsp (1 ml)	ground cinnamon
2	eggs
1 cup (250 ml)	low-fat cottage cheese
¾ cup (175 ml)	low-fat milk
2 Tbsp (30 ml)	vegetable oil
pat of	butter

1) In a large bowl, stir together the flour, baking soda, salt and cinnamon. In a medium bowl, whisk together the eggs, cottage cheese, milk and oil. Add the egg mixture to the dry ingredients and whisk until just combined.

2) Heat a large skillet or griddle over medium heat and then toss in a pat of butter. Pour about ¼ cup (60 ml) of batter into the pan for each pancake. Cook until the pancakes are golden brown on the bottom and bubbles break on the surface. Flip and allow to cook through, about another minute. Transfer to a rack and cool completely. (Yes, of course you can eat them straight away, too!)

3) Store in an airtight container or bag to use throughout the week. You can reheat the cakers in a toaster oven if you're eating them right away or use them straight from the refrigerator to build an easy sandwich to pack up.

QUINOA, BROCCOLI AND CHEDDAR FRITTATA SLICE

In our first book, I shared a recipe for mini quiches that my kids were addicted to. For a solid year, they were happy to have them for breakfast, lunch or dinner. Then they turned on them like the fickle beasts they are (my darling fickle beasts!). Consider this frittata slice the 2.0 version of that recipe. Quinoa adds immunity-boosting minerals, fiber and protein. This is so easy to whip up on the weekend, and it freezes and reheats well. Plus, it's so delicious and satisfying that it has handily grabbed the addicted-to mantle. For now. **CM**

MAKES **12** *Servings*	PREP TIME **10** *Minutes*	TOTAL TIME **50** *Minutes*	VEGETARIAN, MAKE AHEAD

1 Tbsp (15 ml)	olive oil
1	small onion, diced
1	head broccoli, thick stems removed and florets finely chopped (about 3 cups/750 ml)
8	eggs
¾ cup (175 ml)	milk
½ tsp (2 ml)	Dijon mustard
1 tsp (5 ml)	salt
½ tsp (2 ml)	pepper
½ cup (125 ml)	grated medium cheddar cheese
½ cup (125 ml)	grated Parmesan cheese, divided
½ cup (125 ml)	uncooked quinoa

1. Preheat the oven to 350°F (180°C). Lightly grease a 9-inch (23 cm) square cake pan.

2. Heat the oil in a large skillet over medium-low heat. Add the onion and cook until tender, about 2 minutes. Add the broccoli and cook until crisp-tender, about 3 minutes. Remove from the heat and allow the mixture to cool a bit.

3. In a large bowl, whisk together the eggs, milk, mustard, salt and pepper. Stir in the cheddar, ¼ cup (60 ml) of the Parmesan, quinoa and the broccoli mixture.

4. Pour the egg mixture into the cake pan. Sprinkle the remaining Parmesan over top. Bake for about 40 minutes, or until the top is golden brown and the egg is set. Let cool slightly before serving. Or cool and then wrap with plastic wrap and store in the fridge for up to 3 days.

OVERNIGHT REFRIGERATOR PUDDINGS

These recipes came about after I dipped my toe back into journalism and conducted a celebrity interview. During our chat, my celebrity best friend revealed her morning breakfast routine, and this easy oat dish was created in the spirit of her brekkie. Its ease inspired me to look for other alternative puddings, and the chia and hemp heart versions were born. Even when my last neuron is firing in the evening, I can muster the energy to put these together, and I'm always grateful in the morning when we just grab, sprinkle with healthy toppings and go. **LK**

CHIA PUDDING

MAKES **2** *Puddings*		**PREP TIME** **5** *Minutes*		
TOTAL TIME *Overnight Plus* **5** *Minutes*				

MAKE AHEAD, VEGETARIAN, PORTABLE, FAST

1 cup (250 ml)	coconut milk
1 cup (250 ml)	plain Greek-style yogurt
¼ cup (60 ml)	chia seeds
¼ cup (60 ml)	unsweetened shredded coconut
1 Tbsp (15 ml)	maple syrup
¼ tsp (1 ml)	ground cinnamon
pinch of	salt

1. In a medium bowl, whisk together the coconut milk, yogurt and chia seeds until the seeds are dispersed throughout. Stir in the coconut, maple syrup, cinnamon and salt.

2. Pour into two small jars, cover and refrigerate overnight.

COCONUT OAT PUDDING

MAKES **2** *Puddings*	PREP TIME **5** *Minutes*
TOTAL TIME *Overnight Plus* **5** *Minutes*	

MAKE AHEAD, VEGETARIAN, PORTABLE, FAST

1 cup (250 ml)	old-fashioned oats
½ cup (125 ml)	plain Greek-style yogurt
½ cup (125 ml)	coconut milk beverage
½ cup (125 ml)	almond milk
¼ cup (60 ml)	unsweetened shredded coconut
1 Tbsp (15 ml)	chia seeds
1 tsp (5 ml)	ground cinnamon
1 tsp (5 ml)	honey or maple syrup
½ tsp (2 ml)	vanilla extract
pinch of	freshly grated nutmeg
pinch of	salt

1. In a medium bowl, stir together all the ingredients until blended.

2. Pour into two small jars, cover and refrigerate overnight.

RASPBERRY HEMP SEED PUDDING

MAKES **2** *Puddings*	PREP TIME **5** *Minutes*
TOTAL TIME *Overnight Plus* **5** *Minutes*	

MAKE AHEAD, VEGETARIAN, PORTABLE, FAST

½ cup (125 ml)	plain Greek-style yogurt
½ cup (125 ml)	coconut milk
¼ cup (60 ml)	raw shelled hemp seeds
¼ cup (60 ml)	fresh raspberries
¼ cup (60 ml)	raw cashews
1 tsp (5 ml)	maple syrup
drizzle of	vanilla extract
pinch of	ground ginger
pinch of	salt

1. Put all the ingredients in a blender and whiz until smooth.

2. Pour into two small jars, cover and refrigerate overnight.

Even the sleepiest head can't ignore the smell of warm things baking on an early morning.

PEANUT BUTTER AND BANANA SANDWICH SLOW COOKER OATS

I wish I could say this hearty slow cooker porridge had something to do with my family, but it doesn't. I made this for myself because I love anything with peanut butter and, on a cold morning, there's nothing better than its creamy goodness mixed into a warm hug of oats. If it's paired with banana—mimicking my favorite childhood sammie—then even better. **LK**

| MAKES **4** *Servings* | PREP TIME **5** *Minutes* | TOTAL TIME **7** *Hours* **5** *Minutes* | MAKE AHEAD, VEGETARIAN |

1¼ cups (300 ml)	steel-cut oats
4 cups (1 L)	almond milk, plus extra for serving
2 cups (500 ml)	water
1 Tbsp (15 ml)	ground flax
1 Tbsp (15 ml)	chia seeds
1 tsp (5 ml)	vanilla extract
¼ tsp (1 ml)	salt
⅓ cup (75 ml)	chunky or smooth peanut butter
1	ripe banana, sliced
1 Tbsp (15 ml)	honey
1 Tbsp (15 ml)	brown sugar

1. Place oats, almond milk, water, ground flax, chia seeds, vanilla, salt and peanut butter in a slow cooker. Give it all a stir with a whisk to break up the peanut butter. Arrange banana slices across the top. Drizzle with honey and sprinkle with brown sugar. Cover and cook on low for 7 hours.

2. In the morning, scoop oatmeal into bowls, add a splash of almond milk and garnish with your favorite amount of almonds, coconut, banana and raspberries.

CHOCOLATE AVOCADO CHIA PUDDING

There's no harm in having a little chocolate in the morning, especially if it's blended with potassium- and fiber-rich avocado and banana. But, honestly, there are some mornings we'd hand the kids jujubes if it meant they'd put on their shoes faster. **LK**

MAKES **2** *Puddings*	PREP TIME **10** *Minutes*	TOTAL TIME **10** *Minutes*	MAKE AHEAD, VEGETARIAN, FAST

2	avocados
1	banana
3 Tbsp (45 ml)	cocoa powder
¼ cup (60 ml)	chia seeds
2 Tbsp (30 ml)	maple syrup
¼ tsp (1 ml)	salt
pinch of	ground cinnamon

1. In a blender, place avocados, banana, chia seeds, cocoa, maple syrup, salt and cinnamon. Whiz until smooth.

2. Scoop pudding into two bowls and serve or scoop into glass containers, cover and refrigerate overnight.

FANCY TOASTS

This food trend got its legs on Instagram but settled into the family kitchen because, really, what is easier and more delicious than toast! Oh, we know, toast with yummy fresh flavors piled up together. This breakfast has infinite possibilities, kind of like how there's an endless amount of times you can ask someone to brush their teeth. LK

FAST, VEGETARIAN

2

Sourdough toast with sliced green apple, crumbled blue cheese and a drizzle of honey

3

Pumpernickel toast with cream cheese, cucumber ribbons, thinly sliced red onion, fresh dill and salt and pepper

1

Wholegrain toast with mascarpone cheese, blackberries and mint

OTHER TASTY IDEAS:
Brioche toast with mascarpone cheese, raspberries and a little orange zest
Sourdough toast with ricotta cheese mixed with lemon zest and honey, sliced strawberries and mint
Multigrain toast rubbed with garlic, a slice of tomato, fresh basil, a drizzle of olive oil and a sprinkle of salt
Rye toast brushed with mayonnaise, smashed sweet peas with salt, crispy crumbled bacon and fresh chives

4
Multigrain toast with avocado mashed with lemon juice and salt, sliced hard-boiled egg, fresh basil and salt and pepper

5
Cinnamon raisin toast with peanut butter, banana slices, coconut, and a sprinkle of nutmeg

6
Whole wheat toast with whipped cream cheese, sliced peaches and a sprinkle of crushed almonds and honey

BLUEBERRY AND LEMON YOGURT PARFAITS

This breakfast started as a summer treat, but because it's so easy to layer and stars antioxidant-rich blueberries, it found its way into our school-year routine. By the morning, the ginger, lemon and sweet blueberry flavors have deliciously mellowed together and are ready to hit the road. **LK**

MAKES **4** *Parfaits*	PREP TIME **5** *Minutes*	TOTAL TIME *Overnight Plus* **5** *Minutes*	MAKE AHEAD, VEGETARIAN, FAST

2 cups (500 ml)	plain Greek-style yogurt
2 Tbsp (30 ml)	maple syrup (or 1 Tbsp/15 ml honey)
2 tsp (10 ml)	lemon zest
1 tsp (5 ml)	vanilla extract
¼ tsp (1 ml)	ground ginger
1 cup (250 ml)	fresh blueberries
handful of	granola or cereal

TIP Bursty-fresh berries not enough for your buds? Try our make-ahead blueberry sauce (below) alongside the fresh berries or as a substitute.

1. In a medium bowl, stir together the yogurt, maple syrup, lemon zest, vanilla and ginger.

2. Fill four parfait glasses or small jars about one-quarter of the way with blueberries. Spoon about 3 Tbsp (45 ml) of the yogurt mixture over the berries in each glass. Sprinkle remaining berries on the yogurt. Add one last dollop of yogurt. Cover with plastic wrap and refrigerate overnight.

4. In the morning, sprinkle each with your favorite granola or cereal and devour.

BLUEBERRY SAUCE

MAKES *About* **½** *Cup (125 ml)*	PREP TIME **5** *Minutes*	TOTAL TIME **15** *Minutes*

1 cup (250 ml)	fresh or frozen blueberries
1 Tbsp (15 ml)	brown sugar
1 tsp (5 ml)	lemon juice
pinch of	ground ginger
pinch of	salt

1. In a small saucepan, mix the blueberries, sugar, lemon juice, ginger and salt. Simmer over medium heat, stirring occasionally, until blueberries begin to burst and break down, 5 to 7 minutes. Break up the berries a bit more with the back of a wooden spoon.

2. Let cool. Store, covered, in the refrigerator until ready to use.

FRUIT STICKS WITH CARDAMOM SAUCE

If you mix up the dressing ahead of time, you can just drizzle it on your favorite fruit, giving its natural sweetness a lovely zing. Plus, this is such a snappy dish, it gives you time to find that permission slip you've just been told you need to sign. **LK**

MAKES 4 *Servings*	**PREP TIME** 15 *Minutes*	**TOTAL TIME** 15 *Minutes*	MAKE AHEAD, VEGETARIAN

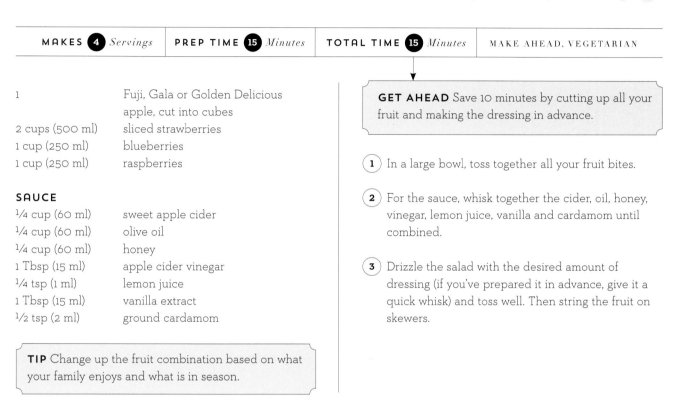

1   Fuji, Gala or Golden Delicious
                            apple, cut into cubes
2 cups (500 ml)   sliced strawberries
1 cup (250 ml)   blueberries
1 cup (250 ml)   raspberries

SAUCE
¼ cup (60 ml)   sweet apple cider
¼ cup (60 ml)   olive oil
¼ cup (60 ml)   honey
1 Tbsp (15 ml)   apple cider vinegar
¼ tsp (1 ml)   lemon juice
1 Tbsp (15 ml)   vanilla extract
½ tsp (2 ml)   ground cardamom

GET AHEAD Save 10 minutes by cutting up all your fruit and making the dressing in advance.

1 In a large bowl, toss together all your fruit bites.

2 For the sauce, whisk together the cider, oil, honey, vinegar, lemon juice, vanilla and cardamom until combined.

3 Drizzle the salad with the desired amount of dressing (if you've prepared it in advance, give it a quick whisk) and toss well. Then string the fruit on skewers.

TIP Change up the fruit combination based on what your family enjoys and what is in season.

PANCAKE TACOS OR WAFFLE SANDWICHES

Marketing is one of those things you need in your back pocket as a parent. And leftovers are what you need in your refrigerator when Monday rolls around. If you make extra waffles or pancakes on the weekend, use the leftovers to dazzle your kids with these breakfast lovelies. We swear they'll brush their hair faster if you do. **LK**

For our pancake and waffle recipe, see our easy, make-ahead Whole Grain Pancake and Waffle Mix on p. 9.

MAKE AHEAD, FAST, VEGETARIAN

HERE ARE SOME OF OUR FAVORITE TACO TOPPING COMBINATIONS.

Cream cheese with sliced peaches,
a drizzle of honey, chopped pecans
Ricotta cheese with sliced strawberries,
a drizzle of honey
Sliced banana and strawberries,
a few dollops of Greek-style yogurt,
a sprinkle of cinnamon

All-natural peanut butter, sliced bananas,
a drizzle of honey, a sprinkle of shaved almonds
All-natural peanut butter, raspberries and coconut
All-natural almond butter, sliced apples,
a drizzle of maple syrup, a sprinkle of cinnamon

Pancakes are great for breakfast. Duh. But we've been known to use leftover cakes to make sandwiches for lunches, too.

MUSHROOM EGG MELT

This melt takes about five minutes longer to make than straight-ahead fried eggs, but the result is approximately five hundred times more delicious. Plus, the protein in the eggs will keep your kids going all morning long. It's a great breakfast for a day that needs to feel a bit special. Like, say, a birthday, or a day when Mom is going to make you wear your stupid snow pants. **CM**

MAKES 2 *Servings*	**PREP TIME** 5 *Minutes*	**TOTAL TIME** 20 *Minutes*	VEGETARIAN, FAST

2 Tbsp (30 ml)	butter
1 clove	garlic, minced
2 cups (500 ml)	sliced button or cremini mushrooms
¾ tsp (4 ml)	fresh thyme
½ cup (125 ml)	grated Fontina or mozzarella cheese
2	eggs
pinch of	salt and pepper

TIP I like to eat these eggs with a side of buttered toast. But you could place the eggs right on your toast or skip the toast altogether. Because, my loves, it's your breakfast.

GET AHEAD Save 5 minutes by prepping your veggies the night before.

1. Preheat the oven to 400°F (200°C).

2. In a smallish oven-safe skillet, melt the butter over medium heat. Add the garlic, mushrooms and thyme. Cook, stirring occasionally, until the mushrooms soften, about 3 minutes.

3. Sprinkle the grated cheese evenly over the mushrooms. Now crack the eggs on top, side by side.

4. Slide the pan into the oven and bake for about 10 minutes, which gives firm whites and slightly runny yolks. Adjust the time based on your egg preference. Sprinkle with salt and pepper before serving.

SMOOTHIE BOWLS

Fun and nutritious smoothie bowls are just as kid-friendly as smoothies but feel more substantial because of all the layers of toppings you can add. Plus, they mimic a bowl of cereal—a childhood classic—without all the trappings of a sugary box of breakfast. Here are three of our favorite bowls to start you off.

 **WATCH** Make a smoothie bowl like a master with our exclusive step-by-step video on sweetpotatochronicles.com.

GREEN GOODNESS SMOOTHIE BOWL

MAKES **2** *Bowls*	PREP TIME **5** *Minutes*
TOTAL TIME **10** *Minutes*	VEGETARIAN

¼ cup (60 ml)	coconut water
1 cup (250 ml)	baby spinach
½	avocado
1 tsp (5 ml)	flaxseeds
1	banana

TOPPINGS

½ cup (125 ml)	sliced green apple
¼ cup (60 ml)	pomegranate seeds
1 Tbsp (15 ml)	puffed quinoa
1 Tbsp (15 ml)	pistachios

1. In a blender, combine the water, spinach, avocado, flaxseeds and banana. Whiz until smooth.

2. Pour into bowls and sprinkle with your choice of toppings.

TROPICAL BANANA SMOOTHIE BOWL

MAKES **2** *Bowls*	PREP TIME **5** *Minutes*
TOTAL TIME **10** *Minutes*	VEGETARIAN

¼ cup (60 ml)	milk or coconut milk
1 cup (250 ml)	plain Greek-style yogurt
2	frozen bananas
2 tsp (10 ml)	coconut oil
	lime zest

TOPPINGS

½ cup (125 ml)	sliced pineapple
½ cup (125 ml)	sliced kiwi
1 Tbsp (15 ml)	raw shelled hemp seeds
1 Tbsp (15 ml)	ground flax

1. In a blender, combine the milk, yogurt, bananas, coconut oil and lime zest to taste. Whiz until smooth.

2. Pour into bowls and sprinkle with your choice of toppings.

BLACKBERRY AÇAI DELUXE BOWL

MAKES **2** *Bowls*	PREP TIME **5** *Minutes*
TOTAL TIME **10** *Minutes*	VEGETARIAN

¼ cup (60 ml)	açai powder
1 cup (250 ml)	frozen blackberries
½ cup (125 ml)	plain coconut yogurt or Greek-style yogurt
¼ cup (60 ml)	pomegranate juice
2 Tbsp (30 ml)	almond butter
1 Tbsp (15 ml)	maple syrup

TOPPINGS

½ cup (125 ml)	fresh blackberries
⅓ cup (75 ml)	unsweetened shredded coconut
2 Tbsp (30 ml)	chia seeds
2 Tbsp (30 ml)	roasted pumpkin seeds

1. In a blender, combine the açai powder, blackberries, yogurt, pomegranate juice, almond butter and maple syrup. Whiz until smooth but not too liquid. You may need to stop once or twice to move things around with a spatula.

2. Pour into bowls and sprinkle with toppings.

"Once, around the holidays, I had a friend bring half a gingerbread house to school for lunch. That's *for real*."

SCARLETT, AGE 10

"I wish you'd pack more treats." JULIAN, AGE 7

"More pasta, please. Like, every day."

ESME, AGE 10

Lunch

BE A LUNCH NINJA

The grind of making school lunches is well documented. By the time both of my kids were in school full time, an endless conveyor belt of empty lunch boxes appeared before me, and I realized I needed an approach to packing lunches. An approach and an attitude.

My preference is to make lunch at the same time that I'm making dinner. I put the lunch boxes out on the counter as I'm cooking and just fill them up as I go. If I'm peeling carrots to go with dinner, I'll prep some extras for the lunches. While I wait for the water to boil for the pasta, I'll pull Broccoli and Cheese Patties out of the freezer and tuck them into the lunch boxes. And so on. By the time the kitchen is tidied up after dinner, I'm completely done. (The exception to this rule is sandwiches, which don't hold up overnight. If I'm making a sandwich, I do it in the morning.) The system worked so well that I started to jokingly refer to myself as the Lunch Ninja. My kids never did embrace the name, but Laura appreciated it enough that we created a video series to help all the Lunch Ninjas out there with lunch combination ideas. Oh, and if you feel more like a ninja making lunches in the morning, that's great, too.

If lunch packing has you feeling flustered, don't worry, I'm going to teach you how you, too, can be a ninja. **CM**

1 WHAT'S THE MAGIC FORMULA? A lunch should contain at least three out of the four food groups: fruits and vegetables, dairy or an alternative, protein, and grains.

2 HOW MUCH? The size of your kid's lunch largely depends on their age, size and activity level. As a rough guide, consider that lunch should account for just less than one-third of the day's nutrition. For example, your seven-year-old could have an orange and 1/2 cup (125 ml) of carrots, a whole wheat pita, 2 ounces (60 g) of cooked chicken and a cup of milk. Meanwhile, your ten-year-old might take an apple, 1/2 cup (125 ml) of baked potato wedges, a yogurt cup, a tuna sandwich on whole grain bread with cheese, and a granola bar. Of course appetites vary from child to child, so talk it over with your kids. If the lunch box regularly comes home empty, ask if they're still hungry after lunch. If lots of lunch is coming home every day, then ask if you're packing too much.

3 WHAT SHOULD I PACK? This chapter will give you lots of ideas for things to make for lunch, but remember that almost any recipe in this book can go to school. Whenever we talk to parents who are struggling with lunches, our first bit of advice is to think outside of the sandwich. Dinner leftovers are great the next day, since they're already made and also because they make a nice change for lunch. Lots of things taste better the next day!

4 WILL THE GERMS COME? Yes, my friends, they will. I leave the heavy lifting of full-throttle germ phobia to Laura, but I do know that many food safety experts say we frequently mistake food poisoning for the flu. Luckily, it's not difficult to keep germs at bay. Thoroughly wash all food and drink containers in hot, soapy water each day. Your lunch prep surface, cutting boards and knives all need to be clean before you start. Once you send a lunch off, assume it will not be chilled or heated with anything other than the insulation you're sending it in.

5 **WHAT ABOUT THE DRINKS?** The best drink you can encourage your kids to drink is water. Even mild dehydration can make kids listless and irritable, so always send a full water bottle to school to keep them hydrated, not just at lunch but all day. Milks—whether cow, soy, almond or rice—offer hydration plus other health benefits (all are enriched with calcium and vitamin D, while cow and soy milk also contain protein). Do not be fooled by marketers who would have you believe that chocolate milk and plain milk are interchangeable. Packing more calories and double the sugar of plain milk, chocolate milk deserves to live in the treat category, not the daily, hydrating drink category.

6 **WHEN CAN I MAKE IT?** Do what works for you, but our recommendation is to do it when you're in the kitchen already making another meal so it's not a separate task.

7 **WHY WASN'T THE LUNCH EATEN?** Sigh. We're not going to pretend this isn't a tough one. Every school has a different way of handling lunchtime. Some kids stay in their classrooms, some have a cafeteria and some eat in a gym that converts to a lunchroom. In most cases, it's loud and chaotic, which may be kind of fun but it's not the best backdrop for relaxed dining. Most schools have rules about not trading lunches because of allergies, but we all know it happens. Don't underestimate the power of telling your kids that you want them to eat their lunch. Many schools have had success with the "reverse lunch" approach, whereby kids go out and play first, then return inside to eat. They have a chance to build up an appetite and aren't in such a rush to get outside that they leave their lunch untouched.

8 **CAN THEY MAKE THEIR OWN @*?! LUNCH?** Whether it's planning or actually making the lunch, get kids involved in any way you can. Not only will it lighten your load; it will increase the chances of that lunch getting eaten.

FANCY TUNA WRAP

My kids have never been big fans of the traditional sandwich. Sushi, on the other hand, was a hit with them from an early age, which is probably why I got in the habit of creating wraps of all kinds—Esme and Julian are just more likely to try things in that format. Veggies I know they'd reject in a regular old sammie I can pack into a wrap like this one, no problem. **CM**

MAKES **2** *Wraps*	PREP TIME **15** *Minutes*	TOTAL TIME **15** *Minutes*	MAKE AHEAD

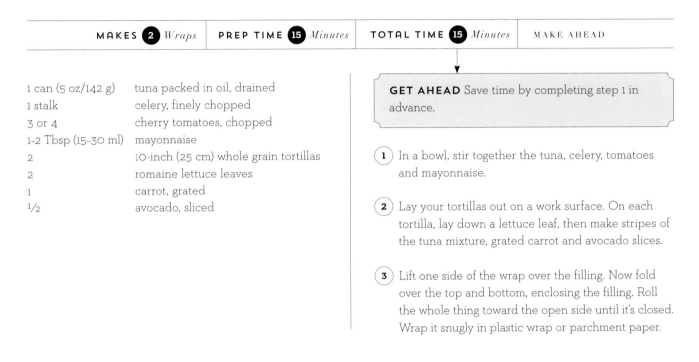

1 can (5 oz/142 g)	tuna packed in oil, drained
1 stalk	celery, finely chopped
3 or 4	cherry tomatoes, chopped
1–2 Tbsp (15–30 ml)	mayonnaise
2	10-inch (25 cm) whole grain tortillas
2	romaine lettuce leaves
1	carrot, grated
½	avocado, sliced

GET AHEAD Save time by completing step 1 in advance.

1. In a bowl, stir together the tuna, celery, tomatoes and mayonnaise.

2. Lay your tortillas out on a work surface. On each tortilla, lay down a lettuce leaf, then make stripes of the tuna mixture, grated carrot and avocado slices.

3. Lift one side of the wrap over the filling. Now fold over the top and bottom, enclosing the filling. Roll the whole thing toward the open side until it's closed. Wrap it snugly in plastic wrap or parchment paper.

TIP Remember, there's nothing stopping you from packing your own healthy lunch while making one for your kids.

CURRIED CHICKEN AND GRAPE POCKETS

This pita sandwich is a bit of a show-off, but you can hardly blame it when it's so juicy, crunchy, sweet and ever-so-slightly spicy. It makes a terrific midterm replacement when the classics are losing their luster. (We still love you, PB&J and ham and cheese!) **CM**

MAKES **4** *Pita Sandwiches*	PREP TIME **15** *Minutes*	TOTAL TIME **15** *Minutes*	MAKE AHEAD

2 cups (500 ml)	diced cooked chicken
2 stalks	celery, finely diced
1	green onion, thinly sliced
½ cup (125 ml)	seedless grapes, quartered
2 Tbsp (30 ml)	mayonnaise
2 Tbsp (30 ml)	plain Greek-style yogurt
1 tsp (5 ml)	curry powder
1 tsp (5 ml)	Dijon mustard
pinch of	salt and pepper
	torn lettuce
2	whole wheat pita pockets, sliced in half

You can use leftover cooked chicken or rotisserie chicken, or poach your own thighs or breasts. To poach your own, place your meat in an inch or so of simmering water that's been seasoned with salt and toss in a few pieces of chopped celery, carrot and onion to add a bit of flavor. Put a lid on it and let it simmer away until the chicken is cooked through, about 10 minutes for breasts, about 12 minutes for bone-in thighs. Either way, cut into the meat to be sure it is completely cooked.

GET AHEAD 10 minutes by poaching the chicken in advance. Save another 5 minutes by completing step 1 in advance.

1) In a medium bowl, toss together the chicken, celery, green onion and grapes. In a small bowl, stir together the mayo, yogurt, curry powder and mustard. Stir this into the chicken mixture. Taste to check seasoning before adding salt and pepper.

2) Tuck a few pieces of lettuce into each pita half, then spoon in your chicken salad. Wrap each pita in plastic wrap before packing into a lunch box.

AVOCADO EGG SALAD SANDWICH

The avocado is a small but significant upgrade to the standby egg salad—it makes the creamiest sandwich ever. It also weaves in the fiber, potassium and healthy fats that make avocado a superfood. Avocado is also known for creating that satisfied feeling, making it a great addition to an active kid's lunch. **CM**

| **MAKES** **2** *or* **3** *Sandwiches* | **PREP TIME** **20** *Minutes* | **TOTAL TIME** **20** *Minutes* | MAKE AHEAD, VEGETARIAN |

3	eggs
2	avocados, pitted
2 Tbsp (30 ml)	finely chopped chives
1 Tbsp (15 ml)	plain Greek-style yogurt
1 tsp (5 ml)	lemon juice
¼ tsp (1 ml)	Dijon mustard
pinch of	salt and pepper
4–6 slices	whole grain bread

GET AHEAD Save 15 minutes by completing Step 1—just don't chop the eggs in advance. Hard boiled eggs keep in the fridge for 1 week.

1. Put eggs in a pot of cold water and place over medium-high heat. As soon as the water boils, place the lid on the pot, turn off the heat and let sit for 12 minutes. Drain the eggs and rinse under cold water to cool them down enough to peel. Remove the shells and chop the boiled eggs.

2. In a medium bowl, mash the avocados with a fork until they're chunky-smooth—you don't want a purée. Add the chopped eggs, chives, yogurt, lemon juice and mustard and give it all a good mix. Taste before adding salt and pepper.

3. Spread your mixture on the bread and top with anything else your kids enjoy, like lettuce or cucumber. Slice in half on the diagonal (every single child's preference) and wrap snugly in plastic wrap.

TIP Whether you're making this filling ahead or right before packing up lunch, be sure to place plastic wrap right against the mixture or flush against the sandwich to stop the avocado from browning.

TIP You could just use one type of pepper, but mixing up red, yellow and orange makes it extra pretty.

PEPERONATA

This sweet pepper mixture can be tossed with freshly cooked pasta or added to a frittata or pizza or, yes, layered with a thick schmear of cream cheese for a sandwich. Or, best idea, all of the above, since this recipe yields such a big batch of luscious peppers. **CM**

MAKES 3 *Cups (750 ml)*	**PREP TIME** 40 *Minutes*	**TOTAL TIME** 40 *Minutes*	VEGETARIAN, MAKE AHEAD

2 tsp (10 ml)	olive oil
1	onion, cut into thin lengthwise strips
6	sweet peppers, cut into thin strips
1 tsp (5 ml)	sugar
1 sprig	fresh thyme
1 sprig	fresh rosemary
1 tsp (5 ml)	coarse salt
¼ tsp (1 ml)	freshly ground black pepper
1 Tbsp (15 ml)	balsamic vinegar

GET AHEAD Save 5 minutes by prepping your veg ahead.

1. Heat the oil in a large skillet over medium heat. Add the onions and cook for about 3 minutes, until they start to soften. Toss in the peppers, sugar, herb sprigs, salt and pepper and stir until everything is well coated. Place a lid on your pan and reduce the heat to low. Allow the vegetables to sweat, stirring occasionally, for about 30 minutes, until they are very soft.

2. Take the lid off the pan and raise the heat to medium. Cook off the excess liquid, which will take about 3 more minutes. Stir in the balsamic vinegar and remove from the heat. Pluck out the rosemary and thyme twigs. Peperonata will keep in an airtight container in the fridge for up to 5 days.

TUNA AND BLACK BEAN WRAP

"I'm so bored of [insert complaint here] in my lunch." I hear it, I know you hear it. How I envy those parents whose kids will eat the same lunch every day for a school year! This tasty wrap is my response to a recent letter to management. It's hearty and filled with protein, but with the lime and peppers, it still feels light. And I'm careful not to make it too many times in a row, so it never gets on the "I'm bored" list. Because I'm smart like that. **CM**

MAKES **4** *Wraps*	**PREP TIME** **40** *Minutes*	**TOTAL TIME** **45** *Minutes*	MAKE AHEAD

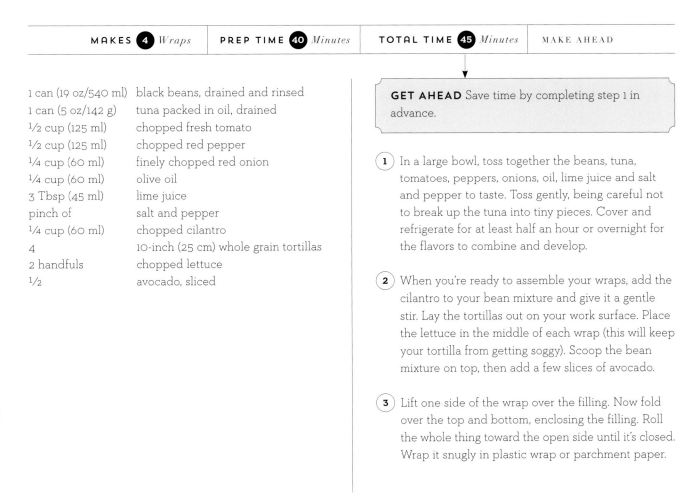

1 can (19 oz/540 ml)	black beans, drained and rinsed
1 can (5 oz/142 g)	tuna packed in oil, drained
½ cup (125 ml)	chopped fresh tomato
½ cup (125 ml)	chopped red pepper
¼ cup (60 ml)	finely chopped red onion
¼ cup (60 ml)	olive oil
3 Tbsp (45 ml)	lime juice
pinch of	salt and pepper
¼ cup (60 ml)	chopped cilantro
4	10-inch (25 cm) whole grain tortillas
2 handfuls	chopped lettuce
½	avocado, sliced

GET AHEAD Save time by completing step 1 in advance.

1. In a large bowl, toss together the beans, tuna, tomatoes, peppers, onions, oil, lime juice and salt and pepper to taste. Toss gently, being careful not to break up the tuna into tiny pieces. Cover and refrigerate for at least half an hour or overnight for the flavors to combine and develop.

2. When you're ready to assemble your wraps, add the cilantro to your bean mixture and give it a gentle stir. Lay the tortillas out on your work surface. Place the lettuce in the middle of each wrap (this will keep your tortilla from getting soggy). Scoop the bean mixture on top, then add a few slices of avocado.

3. Lift one side of the wrap over the filling. Now fold over the top and bottom, enclosing the filling. Roll the whole thing toward the open side until it's closed. Wrap it snugly in plastic wrap or parchment paper.

SHAKE UP YOUR LUNCH SIDES

Friends, we wish with everything that is holy that the recipes in this chapter (and throughout the whole book) are everything you need to pack a balanced school lunch. But we all know that's not the case. Coming up with ideas for "the rest of lunch" can drive even the most creative among us to lunch-making burnout by mid-October. Since you already know you can pack carrot sticks in a lunch, we've rounded up some of our favorite, slightly less traditional lunch box fillers. CM

Bok choy
Beet Hummus *(page 184)*
Leftover waffles with syrup *(page 9)*
Blackberries and kiwi

Mini blueberry bagel with melon balls
    and pomegranate seeds
Sea asparagus, cornichon pickles
    and pickled onions
Mini corn and radishes
Greek-style yogurt with dried banana,
    apricot and coconut

Mini leftover Protein Pancakes
  with Cottage Cheese (*page 33*)
Watermelon, raspberries, pineapple
Popcorn and seaweed
Edamame, cherry tomatoes, bocconcini

Roasted potatoes and sugar snap peas
Hard-boiled egg
Tomato, cucumber and feta pasta salad
Dragon fruit and mango

MORE IS MORE
Drinks: water, milk, smoothies
Fruit: apricots, clementines, persimmons, plums,
  plantain chips, starfruit, cherries
Vegetables: cooked beet cubes, steamed green beans,
  cooked asparagus, olives, lupini beans
Grains: puffed brown rice, whole grain breadsticks, naan
Protein: cooked quinoa, kefir, roasted chickpeas

SWEET POTATO
AND APPLE
(page 70)

MUSHROOM
AND BARLEY
(page 71)

LEMON CHICKEN ORZO
(page 72)

COCONUT LENTIL
(page 73)

SOUPS

S oups are the quintessential school-year go-to. They're easily made in advance. In fact, they taste better when they are. You can pack them with healthy ingredients your kid may not be so happy to see on a plate. And they rock the have-it-for-dinner-then-send-leftovers-to-school thing like nobody's business. Knowing you're sending along a warm, healthy thermos is going to give both you and your kid a good feeling. We don't like to play favorites, but these four soups get high marks for never coming home untouched.

SWEET POTATO AND APPLE SOUP

Promise you'll make this soup, because it's the tastiest soup I've ever made. I know I'm overselling it, but it's always met with a roaring "holy yum!" From the humble school thermos, tripled for a teacher's potluck, doubled for a dinner party and, finally, making a gorgeous debut at my annual Christmas party, where it was sprinkled with pomegranate seeds and chopped rosemary, it is versatile and chirpy with its bright orange hue shining up from the bowl. **LK**

MAKES 6 to 8 *Servings*	PREP TIME 30 *Minutes*	TOTAL TIME 55 *Minutes*	MAKE AHEAD

2	large sweet potatoes (preferably Jewel), peeled and cut into ½-inch (1.25 cm) cubes
4 Tbsp (60 ml)	olive oil, divided
½ tsp (2 ml)	salt
2 cloves	garlic, minced
2	carrots, diced
2	onions, diced
6 cups (1.5 L)	chicken stock, plus more if necessary
4	Gala, Fuji or Red Delicious apples, peeled and diced
1 tsp (5 ml)	ground cinnamon
¼ tsp (1ml)	grated nutmeg
¼ tsp (1 ml)	ground ginger
1 cup (250 ml)	coconut milk beverage
	salt to taste

TIP You can sub in 4 cups (1 L) diced butternut squash for the sweet potato. To make this dish vegetarian, use vegetable stock instead of chicken. For a richer version for a special occasion, sub heavy cream or full-fat coconut milk for the coconut milk beverage.

GET AHEAD Save 20 minutes by doing steps 1 and 2 in advance. Store cooked sweet potato in a plastic bag in the fridge.

1) Preheat the oven to 400°F (200°C). Grease a baking sheet.

2) In a large bowl, toss the sweet potato with 2 Tbsp (30 ml) of the oil and the salt. Spread out on the baking sheet. Roast for 15 to 20 minutes, or until potatoes are fork-tender.

3) Meanwhile, in a large pot over medium heat, add the remaining 2 Tbsp (30 ml) oil as well as the garlic, carrots and onions. Cook, stirring frequently, until onions are translucent and carrot is crisp-tender, about 10 minutes. Stir in the chicken stock, then add the sweet potatoes, apples, cinnamon, nutmeg and ginger. Cover and simmer for about 15 minutes, or until apples are tender.

4) Remove from the heat and, using an immersion blender or working in batches in a blender, purée the soup until smooth. Add additional stock if you want a thinner soup.

5) Return the soup to the pot and stir in the coconut milk beverage. Bring to a simmer over low heat and simmer for 5 minutes. Season to taste.

MUSHROOM AND BARLEY SOUP

I love the texture of barley in soups. It adds heft the way a noodle does but that extra bit of chewiness in the grain makes soups especially hearty. A thermos full of this beauty is just the thing on a snow-pant-cold winter day. Now if I could just find a recipe for getting my kids to wear their snow pants without complaint . . . **CM**

MAKES 6 *Servings*	**PREP TIME** 10 *Minutes*	**TOTAL TIME** 35 *Minutes*	VEGETARIAN, MAKE AHEAD

2 Tbsp (30 ml)	olive oil
2 or 3 cloves	garlic, minced
1	onion, diced
2	medium carrots, peeled and diced
2 stalks	celery, diced
1 lb (450 g)	cremini mushrooms, sliced
2 Tbsp (30 ml)	chopped fresh thyme (or half that amount dried)
¾ cup (175 ml)	pearl barley
4½ cups (1.125 L)	low-sodium vegetable or chicken stock
pinch of	salt and pepper

TIP Packing soup for lunch is like sending along a hug.

GET AHEAD Save 10 minutes by prepping your veggies in advance.

1. In a large pot or Dutch oven, warm up the oil over medium heat. Add the garlic, onion, carrots, celery, mushrooms and thyme. Cook, stirring occasionally, until the vegetables are softened, 3 to 5 minutes.

2. Add the barley and give it a good stir to coat it. Now pour in the stock. Simmer for about 20 minutes, or until the barley is tender but still chewy. Season with salt and pepper. And you're done!

LEMON CHICKEN ORZO SOUP

This is my easy take on the classic Greek avgolemono soup. Between the orzo pasta and the lean chicken, it's a substantial meal, but the lemon gives it a fresh lightness. I find this means I want an extra bowl as soon as I'm finished my first! This is a perfect thermos dinner for a kid who goes straight from the classroom to the soccer field or ballet studio. **CM**

MAKES 6 *Servings*	**PREP TIME** 5 *Minutes*	**TOTAL TIME** 25 *Minutes*	MAKE AHEAD, ACTIVE KIDS

8 cups (2 L)	low-sodium chicken stock
1 cup (250 ml)	orzo
½ lb (225 g)	skinless, boneless chicken breasts, chopped into bite-size pieces
3	eggs
⅓ cup (75 ml)	lemon juice
pinch of	salt and pepper
small handful	parsley, chopped

1. In a large pot, bring the stock to a boil. Add the orzo, reduce the heat and simmer for 10 minutes.

2. Add the chicken and simmer for 10 more minutes.

3. While that's cooking, crack your eggs into a bowl and whisk in the lemon juice. Using a ladle, scoop out some hot broth and pour a small stream into the egg mixture while whisking. Add as much hot stock as it takes to really warm up the eggs so they won't scramble in the soup.

4. Stir the egg mixture into your soup and cook for another 2 or 3 minutes. Season with salt and pepper. Serve with a sprinkle of chopped parsley. (Before reheating this soup, thin it out with more stock or water, as the orzo will continue to thicken the soup.)

COCONUT LENTIL SOUP

Readers of Sweet Potato Chronicles know of the suffering I endure living within a family of soup skeptics. When I make an amazing pot of homemade soup, the reaction my labor receives is often, "Mmmm, that's good. For soup." But not this soup, my friends, not this soup. The aroma alone is enough to win over doubters, and the Thai-inspired flavors are the getaway you're all craving in colder months. **CM**

MAKES **6** *Servings*	PREP TIME **5** *Minutes*	TOTAL TIME **40** *Minutes*	VEGETARIAN, MAKE AHEAD

1 Tbsp (15 ml)	olive oil
1	onion, diced
2	large carrots, diced
2 cloves	garlic, minced
1 Tbsp (15 ml)	minced fresh ginger
1 Tbsp (15 ml)	curry powder
½ tsp (2 ml)	ground cinnamon
½ tsp (2 ml)	ground cumin
⅓ cup (75 ml)	tomato paste
4 cups (1 L)	vegetable stock
3 cups (750 ml)	water
1 can (14 oz/400 ml)	coconut milk
2 cups (500 ml)	red lentils
big handful of	fresh spinach, sliced into ribbons
juice of ½	lemon
pinch of	salt and pepper

GET AHEAD Save 5 minutes by prepping your vegetables (except the spinach) in advance.

1) In a large pot or Dutch oven, heat the oil over medium heat. Add the onions and carrots and cook, stirring occasionally, until they just begin to soften, 3 to 5 minutes. Add the garlic, ginger, curry powder, cinnamon and cumin. Give everything a good stir and cook for another 3 minutes. Then add the tomato paste and stir again.

2) Stir in the stock, water, coconut milk and lentils. Simmer—do not boil—for about 25 minutes, or until the lentils are tender.

3) Throw in the spinach and stir it around until it just wilts. Add the lemon juice and season with salt and pepper.

MINI FRITTATAS TWO WAYS

We really could have said Mini Frittatas 57 Ways, but then it would turn into its own book. The point is, you can put just about anything you want in one of these little protein-packed lunches. They're a great way to use up leftovers or veggies that are starting to wilt—use about 1 cup (250 ml) in place of the bacon and apple below. And while we're at it, these frittatas make such an easy breakfast (just add toast) or dinner (how about a salad?) that you'll always want to have some on hand. Here are two of our favorite combinations, but let this be just a starting place for your own creations. **CM**

MAKES 12 *Mini Frittatas*	PREP TIME 10 *Minutes*	TOTAL TIME 40 *Minutes*	MAKE AHEAD

1 Tbsp (15 ml)	olive oil
1	shallot (or 1/2 onion), diced
1/2 cup (125 ml)	diced bacon
3/4 cup (175 ml)	grated cheddar cheese
1/2 cup (125 ml)	diced apple
8	eggs
3/4 cup (175 ml)	milk
1/2 tsp (2 ml)	Dijon mustard
1/2 tsp (2 ml)	salt
1/2 tsp (2 ml)	pepper

1. Preheat the oven to 350°F (180°C). Lightly grease a 12-cup muffin tin.

2. Warm the oil in a skillet over medium heat. Add the shallots and cook for a couple of minutes, until they begin to soften. Add the bacon and cook until it's crisp. Using a slotted spoon, transfer the bacon and shallots to paper towels to drain.

3. In a medium bowl, toss together the bacon mixture, cheese and apple.

4. In a large bowl, whisk together the eggs, milk, mustard and salt and pepper.

5. Spoon about 1 tablespoon (15 ml) of the filling into each muffin cup. Then gently pour the egg mixture over top.

GET AHEAD Save 5 minutes by chopping shallots, bacon, apple, spinach and chives in advance. Squeeze lemon over apples to stop browning.

6. Bake for 25 to 30 minutes, until the tops are golden brown and the center of the frittata is set. Allow the frittatas to cool slightly before removing them from the muffin tin. Serve immediately or place in an airtight container. You can keep them in the fridge for up to 3 days or freeze for up to a month.

SPINACH AND FETA: Swap out the bacon and apple for 1/2 cup (125 ml) spinach and 1/4 cup (60 ml) chopped chives. Swap out the cheddar for feta cheese. Sauté the spinach after cooking the shallots or onions. Toss together the spinach, chives and feta.

BAKED TURKEY MEATBALLS

One of the best things you can do for yourself when you begin your lunch-making career is to remember that lunch does not have to mean a sandwich. A few of these little meatball babies tucked cold into a bento box or warm in a thermos makes a satisfying "main" in your little baby's lunch box. Because they're still our babies even though they're at school, right? **CM**

MAKES **18** *Meatballs*	PREP TIME **10** *Minutes*	TOTAL TIME **40** *Minutes*	MAKE AHEAD

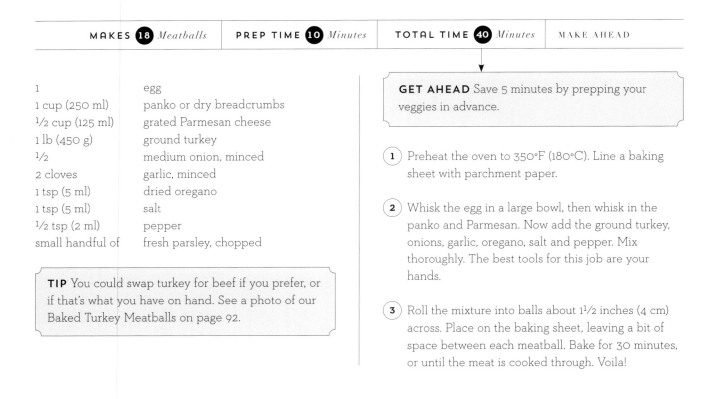

1	egg
1 cup (250 ml)	panko or dry breadcrumbs
½ cup (125 ml)	grated Parmesan cheese
1 lb (450 g)	ground turkey
½	medium onion, minced
2 cloves	garlic, minced
1 tsp (5 ml)	dried oregano
1 tsp (5 ml)	salt
½ tsp (2 ml)	pepper
small handful of	fresh parsley, chopped

TIP You could swap turkey for beef if you prefer, or if that's what you have on hand. See a photo of our Baked Turkey Meatballs on page 92.

GET AHEAD Save 5 minutes by prepping your veggies in advance.

1. Preheat the oven to 350°F (180°C). Line a baking sheet with parchment paper.

2. Whisk the egg in a large bowl, then whisk in the panko and Parmesan. Now add the ground turkey, onions, garlic, oregano, salt and pepper. Mix thoroughly. The best tools for this job are your hands.

3. Roll the mixture into balls about 1½ inches (4 cm) across. Place on the baking sheet, leaving a bit of space between each meatball. Bake for 30 minutes, or until the meat is cooked through. Voila!

The best part
about a
backpack
with a spot
for a lunch box
is that it leaves
a hand free
to hold.
(If they still will.)

SWEET CORN *AND* ZUCCHINI FRITTERS

Fritters have a special place in my heart, since I grew up hitting the New England beaches, where you finish the day with a red-and-white-gingham cardboard container full of greasy fritters made of anything that tastes good with onion rings. These pretty little guys are a great main event for a lunch box but can also be a dinner side or be tucked between a roll as sliders. **LK**

MAKES *About* **14** *Silver-Dollar-Sized Patties*	**PREP TIME** **10** *Minutes*	**TOTAL TIME** **30** *Minutes*

MAKE AHEAD, VEGETARIAN

2 cups (500 ml)	frozen corn
2	eggs
1	carrot, grated
1	zucchini, grated
¼ cup (60 ml)	thinly sliced green onion, plus more for garnish
½ cup (125 ml)	all-purpose or spelt flour
¼ tsp (1 ml)	salt
2 Tbsp (30 ml)	grapeseed oil

1. In a medium bowl, whisk together the eggs and corn. Stir in the carrot, zucchini and green onions. Add the flour and salt and mix well.

2. Heat the oil in a large skillet over medium heat. Drop heaping tablespoons of batter into the skillet. Press down on the batter to form a pancake. Cook until the bottom is golden and crisp, 3 to 5 minutes. Flip and cook on the other side.

3. Drain the fritters on paper towels. Serve with sour cream and a sprinkle of green onions. Fritters will keep for 3 or 4 days in the fridge and up to 3 months in the freezer.

FACT: A lunch packed by a kid is 600 times more likely to be eaten than anything parent-packed. Seriously.

BROCCOLI *and* CHEESE PATTIES

I just feel better going into a school week knowing I've got at least one thing in the freezer that I can pull out to pack into lunches. These patties are often that one thing. They're easy to whip up on the weekend and stand up to the lunch-box bounce-around. Broccoli is an excellent source of vitamin C—important for immunity during school's flu season—so we're always happy to find a new way to tuck it into recipes. **CM**

MAKES 6 *Patties*	**PREP TIME 10** *Minutes*	**TOTAL TIME 35** *Minutes*	VEGETARIAN, ACTIVE KIDS

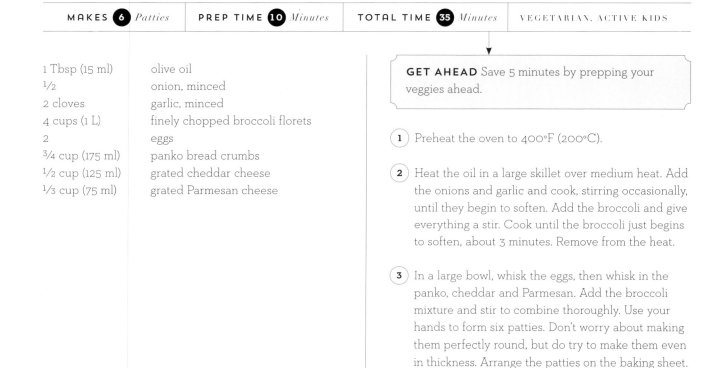

1 Tbsp (15 ml)   olive oil
½   onion, minced
2 cloves   garlic, minced
4 cups (1 L)   finely chopped broccoli florets
2   eggs
¾ cup (175 ml)   panko bread crumbs
½ cup (125 ml)   grated cheddar cheese
⅓ cup (75 ml)   grated Parmesan cheese

GET AHEAD Save 5 minutes by prepping your veggies ahead.

1. Preheat the oven to 400°F (200°C).

2. Heat the oil in a large skillet over medium heat. Add the onions and garlic and cook, stirring occasionally, until they begin to soften. Add the broccoli and give everything a stir. Cook until the broccoli just begins to soften, about 3 minutes. Remove from the heat.

3. In a large bowl, whisk the eggs, then whisk in the panko, cheddar and Parmesan. Add the broccoli mixture and stir to combine thoroughly. Use your hands to form six patties. Don't worry about making them perfectly round, but do try to make them even in thickness. Arrange the patties on the baking sheet.

4. Bake for 15 minutes. Use a spatula to flip the patties, then bake for another 10 minutes. Allow the patties to cool on the baking sheet and then store in an airtight container. They'll keep for 3 or 4 days in the fridge and up to 3 months in the freezer.

TIP This recipe underlines what we say to parents with green-averse kids: cheese is always the answer.

TURKEY, APPLE AND CHEDDAR QUESADILLAS

In our opinion, quesadillas are one of the workhorses of the family kitchen—they're great for cuddling leftovers and perfect for school lunches. When it comes to choosing pairings that make nice with melted cheese, the combinations are endless, but apples and turkey are solid choices in most kids' flavor wheelhouse. And apples and turkey tick off all the boxes of what makes a lunch wholesome and balanced. **LK**

MAKES 2 *Large Quesadillas*	**PREP TIME** 5 *Minutes*	**TOTAL TIME** 15 *Minutes*	FAST, PORTABLE

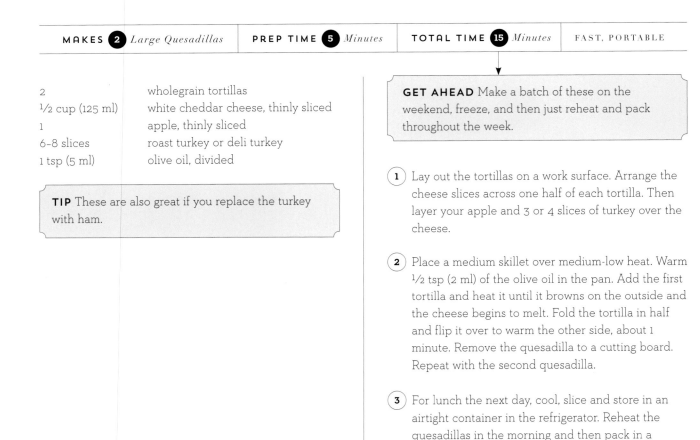

2	wholegrain tortillas
½ cup (125 ml)	white cheddar cheese, thinly sliced
1	apple, thinly sliced
6-8 slices	roast turkey or deli turkey
1 tsp (5 ml)	olive oil, divided

TIP These are also great if you replace the turkey with ham.

GET AHEAD Make a batch of these on the weekend, freeze, and then just reheat and pack throughout the week.

1. Lay out the tortillas on a work surface. Arrange the cheese slices across one half of each tortilla. Then layer your apple and 3 or 4 slices of turkey over the cheese.

2. Place a medium skillet over medium-low heat. Warm ½ tsp (2 ml) of the olive oil in the pan. Add the first tortilla and heat it until it browns on the outside and the cheese begins to melt. Fold the tortilla in half and flip it over to warm the other side, about 1 minute. Remove the quesadilla to a cutting board. Repeat with the second quesadilla.

3. For lunch the next day, cool, slice and store in an airtight container in the refrigerator. Reheat the quesadillas in the morning and then pack in a thermal lunch container.

TUNA RICE CAKES

These meal-in-a-muffin cakes are a frequent resident of my freezer. They make a perfectly portable lunch or dinner for an active kid with their balance of protein, grains and veggies. **CM**

MAKES **10** *Cakes*	PREP TIME **25** *Minutes*	TOTAL TIME **45** *Minutes*	MAKE AHEAD, PORTABLE

½ cup (125 ml)	Arborio rice
1 Tbsp (15 ml)	olive oil
3 cloves	garlic, minced
½ cup (125 ml)	minced onion
2 cups (500 ml)	roughly chopped spinach
1	egg
½ cup (125 ml)	grated cheddar cheese
2 cans (5 oz/142 g each)	tuna, drained

> **GET AHEAD** Save 5 minutes by prepping your veggies in advance.

1. Preheat the oven to 400°F (200°C). Lightly grease 10 cups of a 12-cup muffin tin.

2. Place the rice and 2 cups (500 ml) water in a saucepan and bring to a simmer over medium heat. Cover and cook for 15 to 20 minutes, until the water is just absorbed.

3. While the rice is doing its thing, heat the olive oil in a skillet over medium heat. Add the garlic and onions and cook, stirring occasionally, until onions are beginning to soften, about 3 minutes. Stir in the spinach and let that quickly wilt. Transfer the mixture to a food processor and pulse until smooth.

4. In a large bowl, whisk the egg. Add the cheese, tuna, spinach purée and cooked rice. You want to leave some chunks of tuna, but stir it all together until it's well combined.

5. Spoon this mixture into the muffin cups. Bake for about 20 minutes, or until the edges are golden and set. Allow to cool a bit before running a knife around the edges to loosen them. Store in an airtight container in the fridge for up to 5 days or freeze for up to 3 months.

SPINACH AND BASIL PESTO PIZZA WITH RICOTTA AND SUN-DRIED TOMATOES

If you hear a whole lot of "I'm not eating anything green," take a deep breath, remember these phases always pass, and give this mouthwatering pizza a whirl. This pesto is so addictive it has helped many a kid past the anti-green phase. In fact, I recommend doubling the recipe because you'll want one for your own lunch. **LK**

MAKES **1** *Pizza*	PREP TIME **10** *Minutes*	TOTAL TIME **20** *Minutes*	FAST, VEGETARIAN

1 clove	garlic, peeled and quartered
2 cups (500 ml)	baby spinach
1 cup (250 ml)	basil leaves
¼ cup (60 ml)	grated Parmesan cheese
½ tsp (2 ml)	salt
pinch of	pepper
¼ cup (60 ml)	olive oil, plus more for drizzling
1	large flatbread or naan
1 cup (250 ml)	ricotta cheese
¼ cup (60 ml)	chopped sun-dried tomatoes
½ cup (125 ml)	shaved Asiago cheese
a couple of	basil leaves, chopped, for garnish

TIP We also love making this pesto with kale instead of spinach. Cut this pizza in half or quarters to share between multiple lunch boxes.

1. Preheat the oven to 400°F (200°C). Line a baking sheet with parchment paper.

2. In a food processor, mince the garlic. Add the spinach, basil, Parmesan, salt and pepper; pulse to roughly chop. With the motor running, drizzle in the oil and process until smooth, scraping down the sides of the bowl as necessary.

3. Place the flatbread on the baking sheet. Lightly drizzle it with a bit of olive oil and smooth it across the surface with your fingers. Spread the pesto over the flatbread, leaving a ½-inch (1 cm) border. Drop heaping tablespoons of the ricotta onto the pesto. Top the pizza with sun-dried tomatoes and sprinkle with Asiago.

4. Bake for 8 to 10 minutes, until the edges of the crust are golden brown and the cheese is melted. If you're serving right away, allow the pizza to cool for a few minutes and then sprinkle with fresh basil. For lunch the next day, place cooled pizza in an airtight container and store in the refrigerator. Reheat in the morning, before it goes off to school in a thermal container.

FUEL YOUR ACTIVE KIDS

The older kids get, the more involved they become with the activities they love. As parents, it's amazing to watch these passions develop, but the logistics they bring along with them can be crushing. School ends at 3:20 p.m., hockey practice starts at 4, and the puck drops on a game at 6:30. And dinner is when, exactly? Whether your kid is on the field five times a week or in the dance studio every chance she gets, super-active children need extra nutrition to get them through their long days. **LK**

WHAT YOU NEED TO KNOW

1 CALORIES COUNT. Between the ages of six and twelve, kids need between 1,600 and 2,500 calories each day. An athletic child's appetite is the best guide to how much she needs to consume. You just want to be sure that what she eats is truly fueling her and not just filling her up. For instance, your child will be more energized by an apple with peanut butter than by a bag of potato chips. Like all kids, active children need a range of foods that contain protein, carbohydrates, healthy fats, vitamins and minerals to meet their daily nutritional requirements.

2 HYDRATING IS ESSENTIAL. Every child needs between 4 and 6 cups (1 and 1.5 L) of water a day, and active kids need even more. Children who haven't gone through puberty sweat less than adolescents or adults, so they rely on hydration to cool their bodies during activity. Dehydrated kids are more likely to tire easily, get headaches, have trouble focusing and feel irritable. Kids are also not likely to think of tanking up on water without firm reminders. Make it part of their practice and create the habit: Put on your gear, have a drink of water. Halftime practice, have a drink of water. Changing back into your clothes after practice, have another big drink of water. Work toward a schedule of having them drink 5 to 9 oz (150 to 270 ml) of water every 20 minutes.

Sports drinks, soda pop, fruit juices and punches may hold more appeal to kids than water, but they're also packed with sugar, so consider ways to make water more interesting to your kids, like adding orange or lemon slices for some flavor. (Psst: You can also set a good example by drinking water rather than soda yourself!)

3 CARBOHYDRATES PROVIDE ENERGY. Low-carb diets may be popular with adults, but kids who don't get adequate carbohydrates will tire easily and miss out on the chance to restore the body's main source of fuel. Choose wisely—kids should get their carbs from whole grains such as brown rice, barley or quinoa; fruits such as berries and oranges; and vegetables like sweet potatoes, carrots and squash. Avoid (or limit) refined or sugary carbs like chips, chocolate, candy and baked goods.

4 LEAN PROTEINS HELP BUILD AND REPAIR MUSCLE AND ALSO HELP FIGHT INFECTION. That said, a diet over-weighted in protein is not recommended for athletic kids, because it can encourage dehydration and calcium loss. Kids need 0.5 grams of protein daily for every pound they weigh, so a 70-pound child requires 35 grams of protein each day. Select foods such as chicken, fish, tofu, nuts, eggs, beans, yogurt and lentils. If our kids are going to be chowing down on the go, we like packing up a piece of our Quinoa, Broccoli and Cheddar Frittata Slice (p. 34) with some Trail Mix (p. 180) and edamame. A balanced diet will deliver the protein needs for most kids, so try not to sweat it.

5 CALCIUM AND IRON ARE ESSENTIAL.
Calcium helps build strong bones, and iron keeps energy levels up and balances mood and appetite levels. Be sure your child's diet includes foods with calcium—think yogurt, cheese, chia seeds, oranges, dried fruits and nuts, broccoli and other dark leafy greens. For iron, you can rely on red meat, tuna, eggs, dried fruits, legumes (chickpeas, beans, lentils), spinach and pumpkin seeds.

6 LEAVE TIME FOR PRE- AND POST-ACTIVITY MEALS. Juggling meals with practices and games can feel like trying to run an obstacle course in your bunny slippers, but pre- and post-exercise foods are important. A pre-exercise meal helps to prevent hunger and supplies energy to working muscles, while a post-activity meal assists with muscle recovery.

It's a good rule of thumb to have kids eat 2 hours before exercise. You'll want to focus those meals around carbs, moderate protein, low-fat foods and fluids. Try vegetarian chilis (like our Lentil Chili on p. 158), or fruit, cereal with milk, and yogurt.

Then, 30 minutes after the practice, class or game, children should consume a high-protein snack, like our Nut-Free Energy Bites (p. 170). After 1 or 2 hours, follow up your snack with a high-carbohydrate, moderate-protein meal to help continue muscle recovery. Reach for foods like chicken, fish, meat, cheese, yogurt or legumes (Zesty Chicken with Red Beans and Rice, p. 143).

Although this is an ideal schedule, realities (like bedtimes) may require some commonsense adjustments.

7 ALWAYS HAVE HEALTHY SNACKS AVAILABLE. When it comes to snacks, ease always wins out. In other words, if it's a choice between digging out pocket change from their bag, crossing the ice rink, waiting in line at the vending machine and selecting a bag of chips versus just pulling a container of homemade trail mix from their bag, our bet is on the trail mix. A wide range of items will do the trick: chopped vegetables with cheese, fruits, nut butter on crackers, air-popped popcorn and, of course, fluids.

8 PLANNING EQUALS SUCCESSFUL EATING HABITS. We're a bit of a broken record with this one, but the only way to manage active schedules and meals is through planning. We've spoken to dozens of parents who manage intense dance/soccer/hockey/you-name-it schedules, and the number one rule to survival is always the same. Like your weekly meal plan, schedule prep times for snacks and meals in advance of the other important services you provide, like game shuttle and die-hard fan.

9 GET THE BUY-IN. Talk honestly about nutrition with your active kids. Explain that given the commitment they are making to their sport or art, it only makes sense to support it with a healthy, balanced approach to food. Lots of athletic and active kids will want to do whatever it takes to be faster, stronger and sharper, so why not include them in the important conversation?

School ends at 3:20 p.m., hockey practice starts at 4:00 p.m., and the puck drops on a game at 6:30 p.m. And dinner is when, exactly?

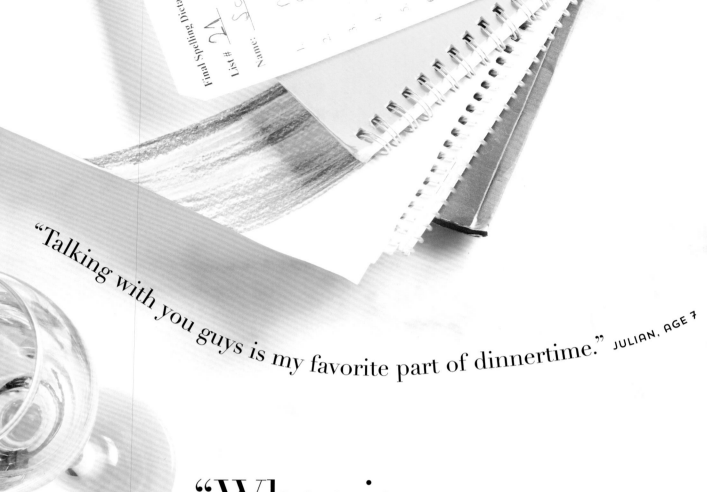

"Talking with you guys is my favorite part of dinnertime." JULIAN, AGE 7

"When is my mom going to realize all I really want to eat for dinner is cake?!"

SCARLETT, AGE 10

"I could eat tuna casserole every night and not get bored."

ESME, AGE 10

Dinner

TIP See Lentil Chili (top left) recipe on page 158 and Baked Turkey Meatballs (bottom right) on page 76.

MASTERING MEAL PREP

Sometimes known as batch cooking, meal prepping is scheduling time each week to prepare some recipes and ingredients for the coming week. Many people like Sundays, after they finish grocery shopping, but you should do what works for you. Next to meal planning, batch cooking is the best thing you can do to save yourself from drowning in the waters of the school week. Think of it as insurance against expensive and nutritionally dubious takeout meals that make their way into our homes when we get overwhelmed. And before you start throwing shade our way, we swear we're not asking you to spend more time in the kitchen—it's actually time you won't have to spend during the week. **CM**

HERE'S HOW YOU DO IT

1 MARK YOUR CALENDAR. You'll need about 2 hours, so carve out the time and write it on your calendar just like any other appointment.

2 MEAL SELECTIONS. Now decide what you're going to make. Of course, any cooking you do now is going to help you out, but you may as well go a step further and get strategic. Check your calendar. See that day with way too much happening? Put that dinner on your list. Got some kids coming over for an after-school playdate midweek? Let's add some muffins to that batch-cooking session. If there's nothing exceptional about your week, just decide on two or three recipes from your meal plan.

3 MAKE SPACE. You need some storage space, so get your fridge and freezer ready for the incoming meals.

4 GEAR UP. Be sure you have enough containers and freezer bags and that they're clean and handy. Pull out everything you'll need: blender, pots, colanders, cutting boards, knives.

5 GET HAPPY. Make things nice while you're working. Put on some music or a podcast. Make yourself a coffee, or heck, pour yourself a glass of wine.

6 AND COOK! Remember to leave vegetables, pastas and grains quite al dente so they don't become mush when they're reheated later in the week.

7 MARK YOUR MEALS. Always label and date everything you make. That way, anyone can grab them out of the freezer or fridge. Depending on who will be reheating frozen meals, you might add instructions for how long to thaw and reheat dishes.

8 MINDFUL STORAGE. As soon as you're done cooking a recipe and you've packed it into its container, get it in the fridge to cool. If you'll be eating the meal within 2 days, you're done. Any longer, and the freezer will keep it freshest. Don't stack just-cooked meals in the freezer, or they won't chill down quickly enough. Instead, spread them out at first. Once they're frozen, you can stack them for greater convenience.

9 DON'T FORGET THE BASICS. Prepping recipe elements can be a time-saver, too. Chop and portion out veggies and fruit your recipes call for (and chop some extra for school lunches while you're at it), dice onions and mince garlic, cook rice or quinoa—you get the idea.

TIP When making any pasta, the cooking water should taste like the ocean—lots of salt.

RIGATONI WITH SPRING ONIONS AND PEAS

When the days start getting longer and the sun sets after dinner, this is the meal you want to eat, since it is fast and simple and uses only five fresh ingredients—which means you'll have more time to play outside. **LK**

MAKES 4 *to* 6 *Servings*	**PREP TIME** 5 *Minutes*	**TOTAL TIME** 20 *Minutes*	VEGETARIAN, FAST

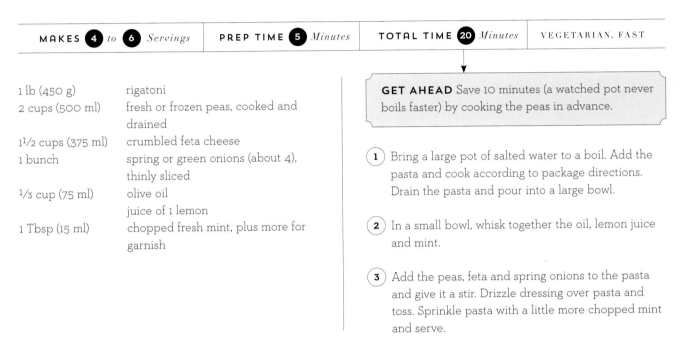

1 lb (450 g)	rigatoni
2 cups (500 ml)	fresh or frozen peas, cooked and drained
1½ cups (375 ml)	crumbled feta cheese
1 bunch	spring or green onions (about 4), thinly sliced
⅓ cup (75 ml)	olive oil
	juice of 1 lemon
1 Tbsp (15 ml)	chopped fresh mint, plus more for garnish

GET AHEAD Save 10 minutes (a watched pot never boils faster) by cooking the peas in advance.

1. Bring a large pot of salted water to a boil. Add the pasta and cook according to package directions. Drain the pasta and pour into a large bowl.

2. In a small bowl, whisk together the oil, lemon juice and mint.

3. Add the peas, feta and spring onions to the pasta and give it a stir. Drizzle dressing over pasta and toss. Sprinkle pasta with a little more chopped mint and serve.

KALE, SWEET POTATO ᴀɴᴅ GOAT CHEESE FRITTATA

You know that feeling you have when you offer to help your kids with geometry homework and then you realize you don't remember a darn thing about what makes a rhombus different from a parallelogram? Well, making this dish has the opposite effect. You can whip together this gorgeous frittata jammed with immune-boosting nutrients (thank you, kale and sweet potato) like a boss since it's so darn easy. Did we mention frittatas swallow up leftovers and make them look like a brand spanking new dish? Oh, eggs, we love you. **LK**

| **MAKES** **4** *Servings* | **PREP TIME** **5** *Minutes* | **TOTAL TIME** **30** *Minutes* | VEGETARIAN, FAST |

1 Tbsp (15 ml)	butter
½	yellow onion, chopped
1 cup (250 ml)	finely diced, peeled sweet potato (about ½ large potato)
1 clove	garlic, chopped
1 cup (250 ml)	fresh or frozen chopped kale
6	eggs
¼ cup (60 ml)	sour cream or crème fraîche
1 Tbsp (15 ml)	coarsely chopped flat-leaf parsley
¼ cup (60 ml)	crumbled goat cheese
	salt and pepper

TIP See how we turn leftovers into frittatas on p. 162.

GET AHEAD Save 10 minutes by prepping the veg the night before or the morning of the meal. Save another 10 minutes by doing step 2 the night before or the morning of. Store the potato and kale mixture in the fridge.

1. Preheat the oven to 375°F (190°C).

2. In a 9-inch (23 cm) cast-iron or other oven-safe skillet, melt the butter over medium heat. Add the onions and sweet potato and cook, stirring often, until softened, about 5 minutes. Add the garlic and kale and cook for another 3 to 5 minutes, until kale wilts and garlic is translucent.

3. Meanwhile, in a large bowl, whisk together the eggs, sour cream and parsley; stir in the goat cheese and season with salt and pepper.

4. Pour egg mixture over potatoes and kale, shaking the pan to help the eggs evenly distribute around the vegetables. Cook the frittata, without stirring, until the edges begin to set, about 3 minutes.

5. Place pan in the oven and bake for about 20 minutes, or until the frittata is set. Turn the oven to broil and cook for 1 more minute, or until the frittata is golden brown.

PENNE WITH SUN-DRIED TOMATOES AND SPINACH

Take it from everyone who has ever made this recipe (and there's lots of them out there, right, friends?!)—it is the bomb. And by bomb I mean a flavor grenade. Loaded with vitamin C, it also lands on the dinner table in record time. In other words, it's the mealtime version of dropping the mic. For those of you not in the know, umami paste is a mix of tomato, anchovy, mushrooms and olives and accounts for this dish's explosive taste. **LK**

MAKES **4** *Servings*	PREP TIME **5** *Minutes*	TOTAL TIME **30** *Minutes*	VEGETARIAN, FAST

1 lb (450 g)	penne
4 cups (1 L)	baby spinach
¼ cup (60 ml)	diced sun-dried tomatoes (not packed in oil)
¼ cup (60 ml)	olive oil
1 large clove	garlic
2 tsp (10 ml)	umami paste
1 cup (250 ml)	shaved Asiago cheese, plus 1 Tbsp (15 ml) for garnish
handful of	basil leaves (about 20), sliced into ribbons

1. Bring a large pot of salted water (it should taste like the ocean) to a boil. Add the pasta and cook according to package directions. During the last minute of cooking, drop the spinach and sun-dried tomatoes into the water. Reserve 1 cup (250 ml) of cooking water, then drain pasta.

2. Pour the pasta and vegetables back into the pot and immediately stir in the oil. Using a Microplane grater, grate garlic into the pasta. Stir in the umami paste and cheese. Loosen up your sauce by stirring in reserved pasta water a tablespoon (15 ml) at a time until you reach your desired consistency. (Sometimes we like it thick and cheesy, so we don't add any water.) Serve sprinkled with additional cheese and the basil.

> **TIP** This dish is also wonderful if you sub arugula or kale for the spinach.

TURKEY LETTUCE WRAPS

This is a great dinner for the final push of the school year. You know, that point when if you have to remind anyone one more time about finishing homework in the evening, not the morning; to put clothes in the hamper, not on the floor; or to *please* bring home that thermos, you're going to lose your mind? I know you know. These lettuce wraps are quick and light, and you eat them with your hands. Which means you don't have to remind anyone to put cutlery on the table. **CM**

MAKES **4** *Servings*	PREP TIME **10** *Minutes*	TOTAL TIME **20** *Minutes*	FAST

1 Tbsp (15 ml)	vegetable oil
1 lb (450 g)	ground turkey
1	red pepper, diced
2	green onions, chopped
1 clove	garlic, minced
1 tsp (5 ml)	minced fresh ginger
½ cup (125 ml)	water chestnuts, drained and diced
1 Tbsp (15 ml)	rice vinegar
1 Tbsp (15 ml)	soy sauce
1 Tbsp (15 ml)	Sriracha
1 head	Boston or Bibb lettuce, leaves separated
small handful of	cilantro, chopped
small handful of	unsalted, roasted cashews, chopped

GET AHEAD Save 10 minutes by prepping your veggies the night before or the morning of the meal. Save another 10 minutes by completing step 1 the night before or the morning of. Store the mixture in an airtight container in the fridge and reheat gently before serving.

1. Warm the oil in a large skillet over medium heat. Add the turkey and break it up with a spoon as it browns. When it's almost cooked through, add the peppers, green onions, garlic and ginger. Keep pushing everything around in the pan until it smells amazing and the vegetables begin to soften. Pour in the water chestnuts, vinegar, soy sauce and Sriracha and give it all a stir. Check that the turkey has cooked through. Transfer the mixture to a serving bowl.

2. Place the meat filling, whole lettuce leaves and your chopped cilantro and nuts all on the table and let everyone assemble their own lettuce wraps. What works best is to make them right in your hand—cup a lettuce leaf in one hand, scoop in the fillings, fold up the leaf and tuck in. It's a bit messy, but that's half the fun.

TIP Swap out lettuce for tortillas if that's what you've got handy.

CHILI CHICKEN BURGERS

Why wait for summer to start grilling? You don't even need a barbecue to make these zesty, juicy burgers. The crema topping might seem an unnecessary step (and by all means skip it if you're too rushed), but it really does take this over the top to burger perfection. **CM**

MAKES **4** *Burgers*	PREP TIME **15** *Minutes*	TOTAL TIME **25** *Minutes*	FAST, MAKE AHEAD

CREMA

1 cup (250 ml)	sour cream
¼ cup (60 ml)	lime juice
¼ cup (60 ml)	chopped fresh cilantro
pinch of	salt and pepper

BURGERS

1	egg
1 lb (450 g)	ground chicken
1 clove	garlic, finely minced
½	red onion, finely minced
1 Tbsp (15 ml)	chili powder
1 tsp (5 ml)	ground cumin
½ tsp (2 ml)	salt
¼ tsp (1 ml)	pepper
4 thin slices	cheddar cheese
4	buns
	lettuce, tomato and whatever else you like on your burgers
1 cup (250 ml)	guacamole

(1) For the crema, in a small bowl, stir together the ingredients. Cover and refrigerate until needed.

(2) When you're ready to make your burgers, put a clean plate on the counter ready to place your patties on. In a large bowl, whisk the egg. Add the chicken, garlic, onion, chili powder, cumin, and salt and pepper. Mix well—you can use a spoon, but the best tools for the job are your clean hands. Divide the meat into quarters, shape into patties slightly wider than your buns (since the meat will shrink a bit) and place on the clean plate.

> **GET AHEAD** Save 5 minutes doing step 1 ahead and store the crema in an airtight container in the fridge. Save another 5 minutes by prepping the veggies the night before or the morning of this meal.

(3) Heat up a skillet or grill with a touch of oil over medium heat. Get your patties in there and cook them on the first side, without moving them, for about 5 minutes until the bottom is firm and brown. Flip them over and cook for another 3 or 4 minutes. Place the slices of cheese on top and cover the pan or your grill to help the cheese melt. When the meat is done, the internal temperature should be 165°F (74°C).

(4) Lightly toast your buns. Spread a nice amount of your crema on the bottom bun, then press on some crisp lettuce. Top with a burger and add some guacamole and your toppings. Carefully put the bun lid on top and you're ready to go.

ORECCHIETTE WITH TURKEY AND BROCCOLI

Whatever your dinnertime problems are, this dinner is the answer. It's fast (the longest part is waiting for the water to boil), there's as much vitamin C-rich broccoli as pasta, and it's so simple that there's very little for kids to push back against. You'll have to restrain yourself from making it more than once a week. **CM**

MAKES **6** *Servings*	PREP TIME **10** *Minutes*	TOTAL TIME **25** *Minutes*	FAST

1 lb (450 g)	orecchiette
4 cups (1 L)	small broccoli florets
3 Tbsp (45 ml)	olive oil
4 cloves	garlic, minced
1	onion, chopped
1 tsp (5 ml)	fennel seeds or fresh thyme
½ tsp (2 ml)	dried chili flakes (optional)
1 lb (450 g)	ground turkey
1 cup (250 ml)	chicken stock
½ cup (125 ml)	grated Parmesan cheese

GET AHEAD Save 5 minutes by doing the vegetable prep the night before or the morning of the meal. Store in an airtight container in the fridge.

1. Bring a large pot of salted water to a boil. Add the pasta and cook according to package directions, about 10 minutes. Set a timer for 2 minutes before the pasta will be done—that's when you're going to add the broccoli.

2. Meanwhile, warm the oil in a large skillet over medium heat. Add the garlic, onion, fennel seeds and chili flakes (if using) and cook, stirring now and then, for about 3 minutes. Add the turkey and cook, while breaking it up, for another 5 minutes, until the meat is browned and almost cooked through.

3. Add the broccoli to the cooking pasta and cook for 2 minutes. Drain the pasta and broccoli and then add them to the skillet. Toss everything together well. Add the stock and toss more. Taste and add salt and pepper. Serve in a big bowl with Parmesan on top.

KALE CHICKEN SALAD WITH BLUEBERRIES

I see you looking at me, all: "My kid will never eat kale." To which I say, "They certainly won't if you don't serve it to them." Stop throwing things at me! Seriously, this is an easy, delicious introduction to the notion of the dinner salad. Creamy cheese, sweet blueberries and tender chicken mean there's something for everyone. **CM**

MAKES **6** *Servings*	PREP TIME **10** *Minutes*	TOTAL TIME **20** *Minutes*	FAST

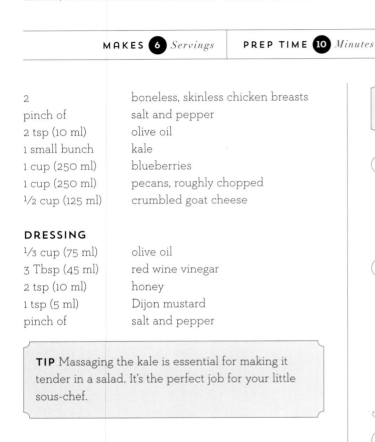

2	boneless, skinless chicken breasts
pinch of	salt and pepper
2 tsp (10 ml)	olive oil
1 small bunch	kale
1 cup (250 ml)	blueberries
1 cup (250 ml)	pecans, roughly chopped
½ cup (125 ml)	crumbled goat cheese

DRESSING

⅓ cup (75 ml)	olive oil
3 Tbsp (45 ml)	red wine vinegar
2 tsp (10 ml)	honey
1 tsp (5 ml)	Dijon mustard
pinch of	salt and pepper

TIP Massaging the kale is essential for making it tender in a salad. It's the perfect job for your little sous-chef.

GET AHEAD Save 5 minutes by completing step 2 the night before or the morning of the meal.

1. You can cook your chicken breasts on the barbecue, in a grill pan or in a regular skillet. Season them with just salt and pepper and cook them over medium heat until they are cooked through, about 5 minutes a side, depending on their thickness. Set aside.

2. Wash your kale, pat it dry, and use a sharp paring knife to cut out the thick rib running down the center of each leaf. Slice the leaves crosswise to make ribbons and place them in a salad bowl. Drizzle the kale with olive oil and toss. Now use your hands to massage the kale. Really get in there and rub the kale between your fingers for 2 or 3 minutes. Don't worry about bruising the kale—this is what makes your salad tender.

3. Cut the cooked chicken breasts into bite-size pieces and add them to the kale along with the blueberries and pecans. You can serve this while the chicken is warm or cooled; both are great.

4. Whisk together the dressing. Pour half of it over the salad and toss. Scatter the goat cheese all over the salad and very gently toss again. Place the extra dressing on the table for anyone who'd like a little more.

SHRIMP AND ORZO SKILLET DINNER

Whenever I'm trying to come up with a new dinner idea, I always assume that I'll be making it when I'm exhausted. So inspiring, right? But if there's a way to use fewer pots and take less time, that's my route to dinner. Exhibit A is this dish that leans on pantry staples, comes together in no time and messes just one pot. Oh, and it's delicious. **CM**

MAKES **4** *Servings*	PREP TIME **10** *Minutes*	TOTAL TIME **30** *Minutes*	FAST

1 Tbsp (15 ml)   olive oil
1   onion, diced
3 cloves   garlic, minced
½ tsp (2 ml)   dried oregano
2 cups (500 ml) vegetable stock
1 can (14 oz/398 ml) diced tomatoes
⅓ cup (75 ml)   balsamic vinegar
                 salt and pepper
1 cup (250 ml)   orzo
1 lb (450 g)   shrimp, peeled and deveined
big handful of   fresh basil, sliced
½ cup (125 ml)   crumbled feta cheese

GET AHEAD Save 5 minutes by doing veggie prep (except the basil) in advance of the meal.

1. In a large skillet, warm the oil over medium heat. Add the onion and garlic and cook, stirring occasionally, until they smell great and soften. Add the oregano and cook for another minute.

2. Pour in the stock, tomatoes with their juice and vinegar. Taste and add salt and pepper. Now stir in the orzo and allow everything to simmer for 15 minutes.

3. Add the shrimp and cook for another 3 to 5 minutes, until the shrimp turn pink. Remove from the heat, sprinkle with basil and feta, and serve.

FAUX PHO

For at least two months of the year I live in fear of the colds and flus whipping like evil spirits through the halls of my kids' school. Science has proved that chicken soup is a legit treatment, and this version is our favorite form of medicine. It's a far-from-authentic pho that comes together in minutes. You can play the spiciness of it up or down, but you must slurp it. Doctor's orders. **CM**

MAKES **4** *Servings*	PREP TIME **10** *Minutes*	TOTAL TIME **25** *Minutes*	FAST

1 Tbsp (15 ml)	vegetable oil
2 cloves	garlic, minced
1 tsp (5 ml)	minced fresh ginger
3½ cups (875 ml)	chicken stock
1 cup (250 ml)	water
1 can (14 oz/400 ml)	coconut milk
¾ lb (340 g)	boneless, skinless chicken breasts, thinly sliced
6 oz (170 g)	rice vermicelli (half of most packages)
6 Tbsp (90 ml)	lime juice
3 Tbsp (45 ml)	fish sauce
2 tsp (10 ml)	sugar
1 cup (250 ml)	julienned carrots
1 cup (250 ml)	julienned red pepper
handful of	cilantro
handful of	bean sprouts

> **GET AHEAD** Save 10 minutes by doing veggie prep the night before or the morning of the meal. Store them in an airtight container in the fridge.

1. In a large pot, heat the oil over medium heat. Add the garlic and ginger and cook, stirring often, until they're translucent and fragrant. Add the stock, water and coconut milk and bring to a simmer. Add the chicken and simmer for 20 minutes.

2. While that's happening, soak the noodles in a large bowl of lukewarm water. Once the chicken has been cooking for 20 minutes, drain the noodles and add them to the soup. Stir in the lime juice, fish sauce and sugar. Taste and adjust seasoning.

3. Serve in large bowls and top with carrots, peppers, cilantro and bean sprouts.

TIP The trick to cooking everything at the same time is choosing small potatoes, or cutting larger ones into small pieces.

SALMON DINNER TRAY BAKE

A complete, hot, healthy dinner and only one pan to clean? Can you hear the choirs singing? This very simple but delicious dinner comes together in half an hour, which is more than enough time to pour yourself a glass of wine and toast yourself for being such a genius. **CM**

MAKES **4** *Servings*	PREP TIME **5** *Minutes*	TOTAL TIME **30** *Minutes*	FAST

12	new potatoes
3 Tbsp (45 ml)	olive oil, divided
2 tsp (10 ml)	fresh or dried thyme
pinch of	salt and pepper
4	salmon fillets (skin-on or skinless, both work well)
1 bunch	asparagus, trimmed
20	cherry tomatoes
big squeeze of	lemon juice

GET AHEAD Save 5 minutes by doing the vegetable prep the night before or the morning of the meal.

1) Preheat the oven to 375°F (190°C). Line a baking sheet with parchment paper. Depending on the size of your baking sheet and your fillets, you may need to use two, in which case put the oven racks in the middle of the oven.

2) Slice the potatoes about ¼ inch (5 mm) thick and scatter them across the baking sheet. Drizzle with 2 Tbsp (30 ml) of the olive oil and sprinkle with the thyme and a pinch of salt and pepper. Bake for 15 minutes.

3) Remove the pan from the oven. Increase the heat to 400°F (200°C). Lay the salmon fillets (skin side down if you're using skin-on fish) over the potatoes and loosely arrange the asparagus and tomatoes all around. Drizzle remaining oil over top of everything. Bake for another 10 to 15 minutes, until the salmon is just cooked through. Squeeze lemon juice over the whole pan before serving.

SALMON RICE BOWL

Fish like salmon is high in omega-3s, which are essential for brain development. But fish isn't always the easiest sell at the family dinner table. A bowl like this one, packed with lots of other goodies, makes it a bit more fun. I adapted this recipe from a restaurant favorite and it's more of an assembly job than anything else. Either use leftover cooked salmon (or any fish your family likes) or start from scratch. **CM**

MAKES **4** *Servings*	PREP TIME **30** *Minutes*	TOTAL TIME **40** *Minutes*	FAST

MARINADE AND DRESSING

½ cup (125 ml)	soy sauce
2 tsp (10 ml)	sesame oil
¼ cup (60 ml)	brown sugar
1 tsp (5 ml)	Sriracha
3 Tbsp (45 ml)	rice wine vinegar

SALAD

3	skinless salmon fillets
1 cup (250 ml)	rice (I like jasmine, but use what you've got)
2 cups (500 ml)	finely shredded cabbage
1	carrot, shredded or matchsticked
1	red, yellow or orange pepper, julienned
½ cup (125 ml)	shelled edamame
½	avocado, cubed
handful of	sliced green onions
2 Tbsp (30 ml)	sesame seeds
1 sheet	nori, torn into small pieces (optional)

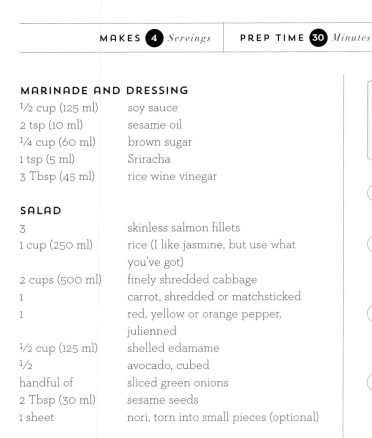

WATCH our video on sweetpotatochronicles.com on how to build your own grain bowl.

GET AHEAD Save 5 minutes by prepping the marinade/dressing the night before or the morning of the meal. Save another 10 minutes by chopping your veggies the night before or morning of the meal.

1. Whisk together the marinade ingredients and set half of it aside for the dressing.

2. Place the salmon in a bowl and cover with the remaining marinade. Cover and refrigerate for half an hour.

3. Meanwhile, preheat the oven to 425°F (220°C). Cook the rice according to package directions, about 20 minutes.

4. Line a baking sheet with foil. Place the marinated salmon on the baking sheet, discarding the marinade, and bake for about 8 minutes, until fish becomes opaque and breaks apart easily. Break the cooked salmon into large bite-size chunks.

5. In a large bowl, toss the cabbage, carrot, pepper, edamame and avocado with the reserved salad dressing. Place a large scoop of rice in each bowl and cover with a large scoop of the salad mix. Top with pieces of salmon and scatter over the green onions, sesame seeds and nori (if using).

SUCCESS:
When you realize everyone is still at the table, laughing, long after the last bite of dinner is gone.

HALIBUT TACOS WITH STRAWBERRY SALSA

There are certain points in the school year when everyone needs a break—the kids are cranky from their schedules and you're over everyone's timetable, including your own. For our family, this point is in May, so I need the help of no-brainer meals to push me through to the end of the school year. This dish is light and fresh and full of omega-3s from the fish and vitamin C from the berries. And it's oh-so-quick. Not that we're rushing. **LK**.

MAKES **4** *Servings*	PREP TIME **15** *Minutes*	TOTAL TIME **20** *Minutes*	FAST

1 lb (450 g)   halibut fillet, skin-on or skinless
1 Tbsp (15 ml)   olive oil
1 tsp (5 ml)   garlic powder
½ tsp (2 ml)   ground cumin
¼ tsp (1 ml)   ground coriander
½ tsp (2 ml)   salt, divided
¼ tsp (1 ml)   pepper
6–8   small corn tortillas

SALSA

1 cup (250 ml)   diced strawberries
1 cup (250 ml)   diced watermelon (the same size as the berries)
¼ cup (60 ml)   finely chopped red onion
1 Tbsp (15 ml)   lemon juice
1 Tbsp (15 ml)   chopped cilantro
1 cup (250 ml)   guacamole

GET AHEAD Save a few minutes of prep time by making the spice mixture ahead and storing it in an airtight container.

1. Preheat the oven to 450°F (230°C). Spray a baking sheet with cooking spray.

2. Place the fish on the baking sheet skin side down and coat with olive oil. In a small bowl, whisk together the garlic powder, cumin, coriander, ¼ tsp (1 ml) of the salt and the pepper. Sprinkle evenly over the fish.

3. Roast the fish until the flesh is opaque and flakes with a fork, 10 to 15 minutes.

4. Meanwhile, make the salsa. In a medium bowl, stir together the strawberries, watermelon, onion and lemon juice. Sprinkle with the cilantro and remaining ¼ tsp (1 ml) of salt and toss. Warm tortillas according to package directions.

5. Flake the fish into large pieces and serve with tortillas, salsa and guacamole.

CAPRESE CHICKEN SKILLET

One spring evening when I was bored with my dinner rotation, I put together this one-pan supper using the ingredients of my beloved summer salad. Maybe it was just me rushing the season, or maybe I was simply trying to get dinner on the table. Either way it worked, and we fell in love. **LK**

MAKES **4** *Servings*	PREP TIME **5** *Minutes*	TOTAL TIME **30** *Minutes*	FAST

6	large boneless, skinless chicken thighs
	olive oil
pinch of	salt and pepper
¾ lb (340 g)	small, multi-colored potatoes, halved or quartered if large
10	cherry tomatoes
½ cup (125 ml)	mini bocconcini
8–10	large basil leaves, roughly chopped

TIP If you can't find mini bocconcini, a.k.a. bocconcini pearls, dice regular bocconcini or about two thick slices of fresh mozzarella.

GET AHEAD Save a few minutes by prepping the potatoes ahead of time.

1. Preheat the oven to 400°F (200°C).

2. Rub the chicken thighs all over with olive oil and generously season both sides with salt and pepper.

3. Heat a large cast-iron or other oven-safe skillet over medium-high heat. Add the chicken, cover and cook until browned on one side, about 3 minutes. Turn the chicken, then add the potatoes to the skillet. Allow the chicken to cook, covered, until browned on the other side, another 3 minutes.

4. Add the cherry tomatoes, transfer the pan to the oven and roast, uncovered, until the chicken and potatoes are cooked through, about 20 minutes. (Depending on the size of your thighs, you may need to remove the chicken from the pan early so it doesn't overcook while the potatoes finish cooking.) Remove from oven and toss in the bocconcini and garnish with basil.

SALMON WITH A BASIL AND SUN-DRIED TOMATO CRUST

This is the dinner Scarlett asks for every birthday, and I never turn her down because it is one of the only ways I enjoy eating salmon. (But please don't tell her I said that.) It's a really beautiful dish—from sweet basil and salty sun-dried tomatoes to the flaky fresh fish. You'll want to make this lovely meal all year round. Kind of like we do. **LK**

MAKES **4** *Servings*	PREP TIME **10** *Minutes*	TOTAL TIME **30** *Minutes*	FAST

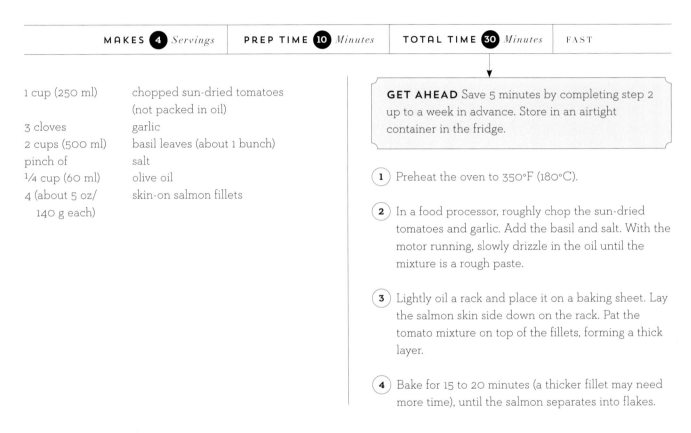

1 cup (250 ml)   chopped sun-dried tomatoes (not packed in oil)

3 cloves   garlic

2 cups (500 ml)   basil leaves (about 1 bunch)

pinch of   salt

¼ cup (60 ml)   olive oil

4 (about 5 oz/ 140 g each)   skin-on salmon fillets

GET AHEAD Save 5 minutes by completing step 2 up to a week in advance. Store in an airtight container in the fridge.

1. Preheat the oven to 350°F (180°C).

2. In a food processor, roughly chop the sun-dried tomatoes and garlic. Add the basil and salt. With the motor running, slowly drizzle in the oil until the mixture is a rough paste.

3. Lightly oil a rack and place it on a baking sheet. Lay the salmon skin side down on the rack. Pat the tomato mixture on top of the fillets, forming a thick layer.

4. Bake for 15 to 20 minutes (a thicker fillet may need more time), until the salmon separates into flakes.

WHITE FISH AND PEA CHOWDER

When I was growing up in New England I never ate the region's famous chowders because, well, to be honest, I was a picky eater. Today, I wish I could slurp up all the great chowders served along the area's coastline. But being miles away from it means that I have to make do with this simple version and sip it alongside my seafood-loving daughter. With oyster crackers, of course. **LK**

	MAKES **4** *Servings*	PREP TIME **15** *Minutes*	TOTAL TIME **30** *Minutes*	FAST

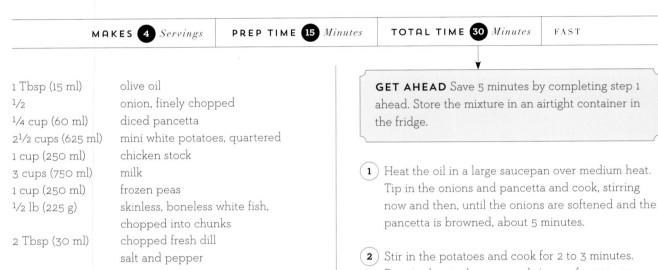

1 Tbsp (15 ml)	olive oil
1/2	onion, finely chopped
1/4 cup (60 ml)	diced pancetta
2 1/2 cups (625 ml)	mini white potatoes, quartered
1 cup (250 ml)	chicken stock
3 cups (750 ml)	milk
1 cup (250 ml)	frozen peas
1/2 lb (225 g)	skinless, boneless white fish, chopped into chunks
2 Tbsp (30 ml)	chopped fresh dill
	salt and pepper

GET AHEAD Save 5 minutes by completing step 1 ahead. Store the mixture in an airtight container in the fridge.

1. Heat the oil in a large saucepan over medium heat. Tip in the onions and pancetta and cook, stirring now and then, until the onions are softened and the pancetta is browned, about 5 minutes.

2. Stir in the potatoes and cook for 2 to 3 minutes. Pour in the stock, cover and simmer for 12 to 15 minutes, until the potatoes are tender. With a slotted spoon, remove half the potatoes from the stock and set aside.

3. Transfer the remaining potatoes and stock to a blender or food processor, add the milk and whiz until smooth. Pour back into the pot, add the peas, fish and reserved potatoes. Cover and gently heat for 3 to 4 minutes, until the fish is just cooked through—don't boil. Stir in dill and season with salt and pepper.

Sometimes we need dinner to do more than feed them— like cheer up a kid who found herself on the wrong tip of a friendship triangle.

TRANSFORMERS

Dear Lovelies, please meet the Transformer Meals. Transformers, please say hello to the busy, hungry masses. You're really, really gonna love these. Why? Because they're your life vest during a tsunami of a hectic week. Yes, we know that's basically every week. Each Transformer begins with a recipe that yields enough extra protein that you can roll it into a new dinner the following night. However, we'll give you two additional recipes to choose from because, if you're like us, having options is always a good thing. The Transformers are designed to make your time in the kitchen more efficient and, of course, oh-so-wonderfully delish.

THIS IS HOW TRANSFORMERS WORK

TRANSFORMER →	*BECOMES* →	*AND* →	*OR*
(1) SPICY BEEF	Spicy Beef Tacos with Roasted Sweet Potatoes	Easy Beef and Black Bean Enchiladas	Coucous Stuffed Peppers
(2) PULLED PORK	Slow Cooker Pulled Pork Sandwiches	Pulled Pork, Caramelized Onion and Sweet Potato Quesadilla	Pulled Pork Burrito Bowl
(3) LEMON THYME CHICKEN	Spatchcock Chicken Dinner	Lemon Thyme Chicken Dinner Salad	Chicken and Apple Salad Boats

SPICY BEEF TACOS
WITH ROASTED
SWEET POTATOES
(page 125)

EASY BEEF
AND BLACK BEAN
ENCHILADAS
(page 126)

COUSCOUS
STUFFED
PEPPERS
(page 127)

SPICY BEEF TACOS WITH ROASTED SWEET POTATOES

The zesty, seasoned beef mix brings a bucketful of flavor to these tacos but is still family-friendly. And never underestimate the power of a taco: they're easy to prepare, versatile and super-fun to assemble and eat, bringing a round of smiles to any table. **LK**

MAKES **4** *Servings*	PREP TIME **10** *Minutes*	TOTAL TIME **30** *Minutes*	MAKE AHEAD

1	large sweet potato, peeled and cut into bite-size cubes
1 Tbsp (15 ml)	olive oil
1½ tsp (7 ml)	salt, divided
½	red onion, thinly sliced and rinsed in very warm water
¼ tsp (1 ml)	sugar
⅓ cup (75 ml)	rice vinegar
2 lb (900 g)	organic lean ground beef
2 Tbsp (30 ml)	chili powder
2 tsp (10 ml)	ground cumin
1 tsp (5 ml)	ground cinnamon
1 tsp (5 ml)	dried oregano
1 tsp (5 ml)	pepper
4 cloves	garlic, minced
½ cup (125 ml)	grated Monterey Jack cheese
handful of	chopped cilantro
	salsa
8	corn tortillas, warmed according to package directions

GET AHEAD Save 10 to 12 minutes by completing step 2 in advance; store the potatoes in an airtight container in the refrigerator. Save another 5 minutes by completing step 3 and storing the onion mixture in the refrigerator. Save a further couple of minutes by mixing up the spices in step 5; store in an airtight container.

1. Preheat the oven to 400°F (200°C). Line a baking sheet with parchment paper.

2. In a bowl, toss the sweet potatoes with the oil and ½ tsp (2 ml) of the salt. Spread potato pieces in a single layer on the baking sheet. Bake for 5 to 7 minutes. Toss, then bake for another 5 minutes, or until fork-tender. Transfer potatoes to a bowl; set aside.

3. In a small bowl, dissolve the sugar and a pinch of salt in the vinegar and then add the onions; set aside.

4. In a large skillet, cook the beef over medium heat, breaking it up with a wooden spoon, until browned, about 10 minutes.

5. Meanwhile, in another small bowl, blend the chili powder, cumin, cinnamon, oregano and pepper.

6. Stir the garlic, spice blend and remaining 1 tsp (5 ml) salt into the beef; cook for another 2 minutes. Transfer half the beef to a serving dish. Put the other half in an airtight container and store in the refrigerator to use for another dinner.

7. Place the beef, sweet potatoes, onions, cheese, cilantro, salsa and tortillas on the table for taco assembly.

EASY BEEF ᴀɴᴅ BLACK BEAN ENCHILADAS

Your pound of leftover beef mix takes on a whole new look when it's paired with an easy fiber-rich black bean dip and rolled into oozy cheese perfection as these baked enchiladas. **LK**

MAKES **4** *Servings*	PREP TIME **10** *Minutes*	TOTAL TIME **30** *Minutes*	ACTIVE KIDS

1 tsp (5 ml)	oil
½	onion, diced
2 cloves	garlic (1 minced, 1 left whole)
1 cup (250 ml)	frozen corn
1 lb (450 g)	reserved spicy ground beef mix from page 125
1 can (14 oz/398 ml)	black beans, drained and rinsed
¼ cup (60 ml)	olive oil
	juice of 1 lime
¼ cup (60 ml)	cilantro leaves, plus extra for garnish
pinch of	salt
10	medium-size corn tortillas
1 can (10 oz/295 ml)	enchilada sauce
2 cups (500 ml)	mixed grated Monterey Jack and cheddar cheese
	sliced green onion
	sour cream

1 Preheat the oven to 350°F (180°C).

2 In a large skillet, warm the oil over medium heat. Add the onions and minced garlic and cook, stirring occasionally, until fragrant, about 3 minutes. Add the corn and cook, stirring occasionally, until it lightly browns, about 3 minutes. Add the beef mix and stir well to combine and warm through. Remove from the heat.

3 In a food processor, combine the beans, oil, lime juice, cilantro, salt and whole garlic clove. Blend until mixture is the consistency of hummus.

> **GET AHEAD** Save 5 minutes and do step 3 in advance and store the bean dip in an airtight container in the refrigerator.

4 Place tortillas in microwave and heat on High for 30 seconds. Coat the bottom of a 13- by 9-inch (3 L) baking dish with a big ladle of enchilada sauce. Spoon 1 Tbsp (15 ml) bean mixture onto each tortilla and spread it across the center. Spoon about 2 Tbsp (30 ml) meat mixture over top. Sprinkle with 1 Tbsp (15 ml) cheese. Fold tortillas over filling and place enchiladas seam side down in the baking dish. Top with the remaining enchilada sauce and cheese.

5 Bake for 15 minutes, or until the cheese melts. Garnish with cilantro and green onions and serve with sour cream.

COUSCOUS STUFFED PEPPERS

A million years ago (read: before I had a kid), I made stuffed peppers with a mix of feta, olive oil and chunks of rustic bread. This version of that dish has been given more heft with the inclusion of couscous. After all, feeding a family is hearty work. **LK**

MAKES **4** *Servings*	PREP TIME **15** *Minutes*	TOTAL TIME **1** *Hour*	MAKE AHEAD

1 cup (250 ml)	couscous
1 Tbsp (15 ml)	olive oil
½ lb (225 g)	reserved spicy ground beef mix from page 125
¼ cup (60 ml)	beef stock or water
4	red peppers
5	green onions, sliced
1 cup (250 ml)	crumbled feta cheese
	salt and pepper

TIP You can sub brown rice, quinoa or barley for the couscous.

GET AHEAD Save 10 minutes by doing step 2 in advance. Store couscous in an airtight container in the fridge for a couple of days.

① Preheat the oven to 400°F (200°C). Grease a 9-inch (23 cm) square baking dish.

② Cook couscous according to package directions. Pour cooked couscous into a bowl and stir in the olive oil.

③ Meanwhile, in a large skillet, stir together beef mix and beef stock. Reheat gently. Remove from the heat and stir into the couscous.

④ Cut peppers in half lengthwise, then cut around stems and chop the pepper tops. (You should have about ¼ cup/60 ml chopped pepper.) Add chopped pepper, green onions and feta to the couscous and stir. Season with salt and pepper.

⑤ Seed the pepper halves, then fill each half with couscous mixture. Place in the baking dish. Cover and bake until peppers are tender, 40 to 45 minutes.

WATCH See our exclusive video on making our grain-free cauliflower couscous on sweetpotatochronicles.com.

SLOW COOKER PULLED PORK SANDWICHES
(page 129)

PULLED PORK, CARAMELIZED ONION AND SWEET POTATO QUESADILLA
(page 130)

PULLED PORK BURRITO BOWL
(page 131)

SLOW COOKER PULLED PORK SANDWICHES

It's amazing what a little cabin fever will do. I created this recipe during a winter that featured a cruel set of temperatures caused by a polar vortex. Then I tested it over the course of a few months' worth of dinner parties with neighborhood friends. I knew it was ready for the world when all the kids in our section of the universe had given it the two-thumbs-up. **LK**

MAKES 8 *to* 10 *Servings*	**PREP TIME** 30 *Minutes*	**TOTAL TIME** 8 *Hours* 30 *Minutes*	MAKE AHEAD

GET AHEAD You can cook the pork a day ahead and reheat in the sauce.

4 Tbsp (60 ml)	brown sugar, divided
4 tsp (20 ml)	salt
4 tsp (20 ml)	chili powder
2 tsp (10 ml)	dry mustard
1 tsp (5 ml)	ground cumin
1 tsp (5 ml)	garlic powder
1 tsp (5 ml)	pepper
½ tsp (2 ml)	ground cinnamon
¼ tsp (1 ml)	grated nutmeg
2 tsp (10 ml)	vegetable oil
1 (3–4 lb/1.3–1.8 kg)	boneless pork shoulder blade roast, trimmed of excess fat, tied
¾ cup (175 ml)	water
½ cup (125 ml)	apple cider vinegar
½ cup (125 ml)	orange juice
3 Tbsp (45 ml)	tomato paste
6	brioche buns

1. In a small bowl, stir together 2 Tbsp (30 ml) of the brown sugar, salt, chili powder, mustard, cumin, garlic powder, pepper, cinnamon and nutmeg; stir well. Rub the spice mixture all over the pork.

2. Heat the oil in a large skillet over medium heat. Add the pork and cook, turning, until browned on all sides, about 10 minutes. Watch your meat and lower the heat if necessary because the sugar in the rub can easily burn. Transfer the pork to a plate. Add water to the skillet and whisk until the drippings are dissolved. Transfer the liquid to your slow cooker.

3. Add the vinegar, orange juice, tomato paste and remaining 2 Tbsp (30 ml) brown sugar to the slow cooker and whisk. Add the pork, cover and cook on Low for 8 hours. If the liquid does not fully cover your shoulder (as is the case with my slow cooker), you'll need to turn it halfway through the cooking time so the other side benefits from the juice pool.

4. Transfer the pork to a cutting board and untie it. Strain the liquid into a Dutch oven or large saucepan and spoon off any fat and keep it warm over low heat. Using two forks, shred the pork into bite-size pieces (or roughly chop). Stir the shredded meat into the sauce. Taste and season with salt. Remove from the heat. Spoon 1½ to 2 cups (375 to 500 ml) pulled pork and sauce into an airtight container and refrigerate for another meal. Serve the remainder warm, piled on brioche buns topped with slaw.

PULLED PORK, CARAMELIZED ONION
AND SWEET POTATO QUESADILLA

Can anything with caramelized onions not be good? No. So there's your proof for needing to make this dish. Oh, and it's full of immune-boosting sweet potato. End of story. **LK**

MAKES ❹ *Servings*	PREP TIME ❿ *Minutes*	TOTAL TIME ㊺ *Minutes*	ACTIVE KIDS, PORTABLE, FAST

2 Tbsp (30 ml)	olive oil, divided, plus a drizzle for the tortillas
1 tsp (5 ml)	butter
1 large	sweet onion, cut into ⅛-inch (3 mm) slices
1 large	sweet potato, peeled and cut into bite-size cubes
1 tsp (5 ml)	chili powder
½ tsp (2 ml)	ground cumin
¼ tsp (1 ml)	dried oregano
	salt
8	medium-sized tortillas
2 cups (500 ml)	grated Fontina cheese
1½–2 cups (375–500 ml)	reserved slow cooker pulled pork from page 129 (depending on how much you like inside your quesadillas)
handful of	cilantro
1	avocado

1. Preheat the oven to 400°F (200°C). Grease a large baking sheet with nonstick spray.

2. Heat 1 Tbsp (15 ml) of the oil and the butter in a 12-inch (30 cm) skillet over medium-low heat. Add the onions and allow them to slowly cook, stirring every 10 minutes, until they are golden brown, about 40 minutes. Transfer the onions to a bowl. (Do not wash out the skillet.)

3. Meanwhile, in a medium bowl, toss the sweet potatoes with the remaining 1 Tbsp (15 ml) oil as well as the chili powder, cumin, oregano and salt to taste. Spread the sweet potatoes in a single layer on the baking sheet, flipping halfway, and roast until golden brown and fork-tender, 20 to 25 minutes.

4. In the same skillet you caramelized the onions, heat a drizzle of olive oil over medium heat. Place a tortilla in the pan and sprinkle with one-quarter of the Fontina, one-quarter of the onions, one-quarter of the sweet potatoes and one-quarter of the pulled pork. Top with a second tortilla. Cook until the bottom of the tortilla gets golden brown and starts to crisp. Carefully flip the quesadilla and cook on the other side until it browns, another 2 to 3 minutes. Transfer to a cutting board to cool for a minute, then slice it into triangles. Repeat with the remaining tortillas and fillings.

5. Serve with a handful of chopped cilantro sprinkled over top and sliced avocado.

PULLED PORK BURRITO BOWL

God bless the grain bowl, because it makes leftovers look like restaurant-quality meals, especially if you follow our easy guide to creating a dinner bowl on p. 163. This bowl has all the appeal of a Tex-Mex supper, just healthier. **LK**

MAKES ❹ *Servings*	**PREP TIME** ❿ *Minutes*	**TOTAL TIME** ㊵ *Minutes*	FAST, ACTIVE KIDS

2 cups (500 ml)	brown rice
1 large	sweet potato, peeled and cut into small cubes
1 Tbsp (15 ml)	olive oil
½ tsp (2 ml)	chili powder
	salt
1	tomato, diced and drizzled with a little olive oil and salt
1	avocado, cubed
1½ cups (375 ml)	reserved slow cooker pulled pork, reheated from page 129

BLACK BEAN AND CORN SALSA

1½ cups (375 ml)	frozen sweet corn, cooked
1 can (14 oz/398 ml)	black beans, drained and rinsed
½	red onion, finely chopped
1 clove	garlic, minced
1 Tbsp (15 ml)	olive oil
	juice of 1 lime
handful of	cilantro, finely chopped
pinch of	salt

CREMA

2 cups (500 ml)	sour cream
¼ cup (60 ml)	lime juice
¼ tsp (1 ml)	chili powder
handful of	cilantro, finely chopped
pinch of	salt and pepper

> **GET AHEAD** Save 30 minutes by doing step 2 in advance. Save another 15 minutes by doing step 3 in advance, too.

1. Preheat the oven to 400°F (200°C).

2. For the burrito bowl, in a large saucepan, combine the rice and 4 cups (1 L) water. Bring to a boil, then cover, reduce heat and simmer until rice is tender and the water is absorbed, about 20 minutes. Fluff with a fork and keep warm.

3. Meanwhile, in a bowl, toss the sweet potatoes with the oil, chili powder and salt to taste. Spread on a baking sheet and roast for 15 minutes. Turn the potatoes and roast for another 10 minutes, or until fork-tender and golden brown. Set aside.

4. Meanwhile, make the salsa. In a medium bowl, mix the corn, black beans, onion, garlic, oil and lime juice. Stir in the cilantro and season with salt to taste. Chill until ready to use.

5. To make the crema, in a small bowl, stir together the sour cream, lime juice, chili powder, cilantro, and salt and pepper to taste.

6. Assemble bowls with brown rice, roasted sweet potato, diced tomato, avocado, the salsa and the pulled pork. Drizzle with crema dressing and sprinkle with fresh cilantro.

CHICKEN
AND APPLE
SALAD BOATS
(page 135)

LEMON THYME
CHICKEN DINNER SALAD
(page 134)

SPATCHCOCK
CHICKEN DINNER
(page 133)

SPATCHCOCK CHICKEN DINNER

I know we're firmly planted in the school year and summer is a distant memory (sigh!), but this is a feast I pull out when I need a crowd-pleaser at our tiny beach cottage. It requires little prep and always delivers. And since it doesn't lean on any seasonal produce, plus gives me miles of leftovers, it was a no-brainer to make it part of my usual dinner roster. **LK**

MAKES ❻ to ❽ *Servings*	PREP TIME ❿ *Minutes*	TOTAL TIME ❶ *Hour* ❿ *Minutes*	ACTIVE KIDS

1	large lemon
¼ cup (60 ml)	extra-virgin olive oil
1 Tbsp (15 ml)	chopped fresh thyme
1 tsp (5 ml)	dried oregano
1 (3–4 lb/1.3–1.8 kg)	spatchcocked chicken
2½ tsp (12 ml)	salt, divided
½ tsp (2 ml)	pepper
1 lb (450 g)	new potatoes, halved
1 head	garlic, cloves separated and peeled
1 Tbsp (15 ml)	olive oil

TIP A spatchcock chicken has had the backbone removed so it lies flat. This can easily be done by a butcher or at home.

① Preheat the oven to 425°F (220°C). Zest half the lemon; juice the whole lemon.

② In a small bowl, whisk together the lemon zest, lemon juice, extra-virgin olive oil, thyme and oregano. Lay the chicken skin side up in a large roasting pan and brush the herb mixture over the chicken. (If you have the time, allow the chicken to marinate in this mix in an extra-large plastic bag for an hour.) Season the chicken with 2 tsp (10 ml) salt and ½ tsp (2 ml) pepper.

③ Meanwhile, in a large bowl, toss your potatoes, garlic cloves, oil and remaining ½ tsp (2 ml) salt. Scatter the potatoes and garlic around the chicken in a single layer.

④ Roast for 40 to 45 minutes, until a thermometer inserted into the thickest portion of the breast reads 165°F (74°C). Let the chicken rest for 10 minutes. Carve—putting some meat aside for your next transformer—and serve with the potatoes, garlic and a side salad.

WATCH Check out our spatchcocking how-to video on sweetpotatochronicles.com.

LEMON THYME CHICKEN DINNER SALAD

This mother of a salad could be its own transformer since it yields so much herby goodness. From the warm, salty potatoes and oozy soft-boiled eggs to the citrusy chicken and crisp veggies, there's something in it for everyone. Unless you're looking for chocolate. Then you're out of luck. **LK**

MAKES **6** *Servings*	PREP TIME **40** *Minutes*	TOTAL TIME **40** *Minutes*	ACTIVE KIDS

4 cups (1 L)	sliced romaine lettuce
2 cups (500 ml)	mini kale
1½–2 cups (500 ml)	spatchcock leftover diced chicken from page 133
2 cups (500 ml)	halved small multi-colored potatoes
	pinch of salt
4	eggs
1 cup (250 ml)	sliced carrots
1 cup (250 ml)	halved cherry tomatoes
1 cup (250 ml)	diced cucumber
½ cup (125 ml)	shaved Asiago or Parmesan cheese
¼ cup (60 ml)	sliced green onions
½ tsp (2 ml)	chopped fresh thyme

CREAMY LEMON DRESSING

¼ cup (60 ml)	extra-virgin olive oil
zest of	½ lemon
2 Tbsp (30 ml)	Vegenaise (I choose it over mayonnaise, but you use what you prefer)
1 Tbsp (15 ml)	white wine vinegar
½ tsp (2 ml)	honey
¼ tsp (1 ml)	Dijon mustard
pinch of	salt and pepper

TIP Don't dress the whole salad, or the leftovers will be soggy the next day.

GET AHEAD Chop the carrots, cherry tomatoes, cucumber and onion the night before or the morning of the meal. Save 15 minutes by boiling and seasoning the potatoes in advance. Save even more time by completing step 2 a day or two ahead.

1. In a large pot of water, boil potatoes until tender, about 10 minutes. Drain and toss with olive oil and salt. Set aside.

2. In a very large bowl, toss together the romaine lettuce and mini kale. Arrange the chicken, cooked potatoes, carrots, cherry tomatoes, cucumber and cheese in groups on top of the salad.

3. Meanwhile, fill a separate saucepan with water. Gently add the eggs. Be sure the eggs are covered with at least an inch (2.5 cm) of water. Cover, bring to a boil over high heat, stirring gently, then remove from the heat and let stand for 5 to 7 minutes. Drain the eggs and place them in a bowl of cold water for a few minutes. Peel the eggs and cut them in half lengthwise. Arrange them on top of the salad.

4. Sprinkle the entire salad with green onions and fresh thyme. Allow each person to dress their own salad.

OR TRANSFORMER (3) CAN BECOME

CHICKEN ᴀɴᴅ APPLE SALAD BOATS

This addictive chicken salad served over romaine halves makes a great dinner or effortless school lunch. And don't take me to task on the cutesy name. I know they don't really look like boats, but throw me a bone here. The kids like the tag. **LK**

MAKES ④ *Servings*	**PREP TIME** ⑮ *Minutes*	**TOTAL TIME** ⑮ *Minutes*	ACTIVE KIDS, FAST, PORTABLE

2 cups (500 ml)	chopped spatchcock chicken from page 133
½	green apple, diced
3 Tbsp (45 ml)	Vegenaise (I choose it over mayonnaise, but you use what you prefer)
1	green onion, chopped, plus extra for garnish
pinch of	salt and pepper
4	romaine lettuce hearts
1 cup (250 ml)	grated cheddar cheese

TIP These boats taste amazing with a drizzle of leftover Creamy Lemon Dressing (p. 134).

1. In a medium bowl, mix together the chicken, apple, Vegenaise, green onion, and a pinch each of salt and pepper until well mixed.

2. Cut each romaine heart in half lengthwise and remove the small center leaves to create a hollow. Spoon chicken salad into the boat halves. Sprinkle with cheese and a bit more green onion.

SWEET POTATO SHEPHERD'S PIE

This is easily one of our family's favorite meals. I created and tweaked this recipe over the course of one of our city's coldest and snowiest winters. It's not a traditional recipe, since it uses a beef base that includes cumin and chili powder, great complements to the warmth of the sweet potato. We love this dish for its comforting quality, and because it reminds us of so many fun nights cuddled together playing board games. **LK**

MAKES **2** *Casseroles,* **4** *to* **6** *Servings Each*	PREP TIME **35** *Minutes*	TOTAL TIME **1** *Hour* **10** *Minutes*	MAKE AHEAD

2 lb (900 g)	lean ground beef
2 large cloves	garlic, diced
3 stalks	celery, diced
2	yellow onions, diced
2	large carrots, diced
2 Tbsp (30 ml)	chili powder
2 tsp (10 ml)	ground cumin
1 tsp (5 ml)	ground cinnamon
1 tsp (5 ml)	dried oregano
1½ tsp (7 ml)	salt, divided
½ tsp (2 ml)	pepper
2 Tbsp (30 ml)	spelt flour
½ cup (125 ml)	beef stock
¼ cup (60 ml)	water
6 drops	Worcestershire sauce
2 large	sweet potatoes, peeled and cut into even 2-inch (5 cm) wedges
½ cup (125 ml)	milk
3 Tbsp (45 ml)	butter

1. Preheat the oven to 350°F (180°C).

2. In a Dutch oven, cook the beef over medium heat, breaking it up with a wooden spoon, until browned, about 10 minutes.

3. Stir in the garlic, celery, onions, carrots, chili powder, cumin, cinnamon, oregano, 1 tsp (5 ml) of the salt and the pepper. Cook, stirring occasionally, until vegetables are tender, about 15 minutes.

GET AHEAD Save 15 minutes prepping all the vegetables before making the meal. Complete step 5 up to 2 days in advance and store in an airtight container in the refrigerator.

4. Stir in the flour and cook, stirring, for 1 minute. Stir in the stock, water and Worcestershire sauce; simmer for 3 minutes. Divide mixture between two 8-inch (20 cm) square or round baking dishes.

5. Meanwhile, in a large pot of boiling salted water, cook sweet potatoes until tender, about 12 minutes. Drain and return potatoes to pot and mash until smooth. Stir in milk, butter and remaining ½ tsp (2 ml) salt; then spread evenly over the beef mixture in both dishes.

6. Bake one pie until bubbly at the edges, about 35 minutes. Cover the second pie with plastic wrap and then foil and freeze for up to 1 month. When it's time to eat it, bake, uncovered and still frozen, at 350°F (180°C) for 50 to 60 minutes.

WATCH Check out our exclusive video for creating Mini Sweet Potato Shepherd's Pie Cups for school lunches on sweetpotatochronicles.com.

TIP This recipe yields two casseroles: one for dinner, one for the freezer. Instead of a second casserole, you can make mini shepherd's pies for school, using store-bought frozen phyllo cups.

EASY RATATOUILLE WITH CHICKPEAS

Vegetarian dinners can get a bad rap for being too light to satisfy certain members of the dinner table (looking at you, dudes). But this one-pan dinner is hearty in a way that won't weigh you down. Perfect on a winter night when you want to go meatless. **CM**

MAKES 8 *Servings*	**PREP TIME** 15 *Minutes*	**TOTAL TIME** 45 *Minutes*	VEGETARIAN, MAKE AHEAD

1 can (19 oz/540 ml) diced tomatoes
1 can (19 oz/540 ml) chickpeas, drained and rinsed
3 cloves garlic, minced
½ onion, chopped
1 Tbsp (15 ml) balsamic vinegar
2 tsp (10 ml) dried oregano
pinch of salt and pepper
2 cups (500 ml) green zucchini cut into ¼-inch (5 mm) slices
2 cups (500 ml) yellow zucchini cut into ¼-inch (5 mm) slices
1 cup (250 ml) eggplant cut into ¼-inch (5 mm) slices and each slice cut into quarters
1 red pepper, cut into ½-inch (1 cm) slices
½ cup (125 ml) goat cheese

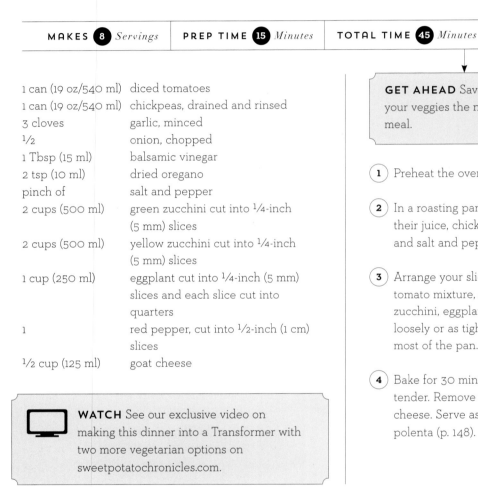

WATCH See our exclusive video on making this dinner into a Transformer with two more vegetarian options on sweetpotatochronicles.com.

GET AHEAD Save 10 minutes by prepping all of your veggies the night before or the morning of the meal.

1. Preheat the oven to 375°F (190°C).

2. In a roasting pan, stir together the tomatoes with their juice, chickpeas, garlic, onion, vinegar, oregano, and salt and pepper to taste.

3. Arrange your sliced vegetables in rows over the tomato mixture, alternating green and yellow zucchini, eggplant and red pepper. Arrange them as loosely or as tightly as you need to in order to cover most of the pan.

4. Bake for 30 minutes, or until the vegetables are very tender. Remove from the oven and dot with goat cheese. Serve as is or over pearl couscous or polenta (p. 148).

TURKEY MEATLOAF WITH APPLES AND SAGE

During the launch of our first book, the media schedule collided with the beginning of the school year, so our days were hectic to the power of 10. In a desperate moment at dinner, I threw a Hail Mary in the oven and the first incarnation of this dish came out. It was eventually perfected, becoming these lovely mini loaves that combine the sweetness of apples with the savory and earthy hit of sage. **LK**

MAKES **8** *Mini Loaves or* **1** *Regular Loaf* | **PREP TIME** **20** *Minutes* | **TOTAL TIME** **1** *Hour* **15** *Minutes* | MAKE AHEAD

1½ Tbsp (22 ml)	butter
3 cloves	garlic, minced
2	shallots, finely chopped
2	Gala apples, peeled and cut into small chunks
⅔ cup (150 ml)	dry or fresh breadcrumbs
⅔ cup (150 ml)	milk
2 lb (900 g)	ground turkey
1	large egg, lightly beaten
¼ cup (60 ml)	apple butter, plus 1 Tbsp (15 ml) for tops of loaves
2 Tbsp (30 ml)	chopped fresh sage
1 tsp (5 ml)	fine sea salt
¼ tsp (1 ml)	pepper

GET AHEAD Save 5 minutes by prepping your apples (and giving them a squeeze of lemon to prevent browning) and veggies the night before or the morning of the meal.

1. Preheat the oven to 400°F (200°C). Grease eight mini loaf pans or a small baking pan.

2. In a medium skillet, melt the butter over medium heat. Add the garlic and shallots and cook, stirring occasionally, until the shallots are softened, about 3 minutes.

3. In a large bowl, stir together the apple chunks, breadcrumbs and milk; allow to soak for about 5 minutes. Add your turkey and mix to combine. Stir in the egg as well as the garlic and shallot mixture, being sure to scrape all the butter from the pan into the bowl. Add the apple butter, sage, salt and pepper and mix evenly. Spoon the meat mixture into the loaf pans. If you're not using mini loaf pans, place your meat on the baking sheet and shape it into an oval.

4. Bake for about 50 minutes, or until the internal temperature of a loaf reaches 160°F (71°C). In the last few minutes of the cooking, brush the tops with apple butter. Allow the loaves to rest for 5 minutes before serving.

Weeknight dinner traditions are the makings of lifelong food memories.

BAKED FRIED CHICKEN

Sometimes we need dinner to do a bit more than avert an impending blood sugar crash—like cheer up a kid who found herself on the wrong tip of a friendship triangle that day. If a recipe could give a hug, this would be that dinner. There's something essentially comforting about fried chicken, but we couldn't help ourselves from making this one a bit healthier. Serve with a side of understanding. Mashed potatoes wouldn't hurt either. **CM**

MAKES 4 *Servings*	**PREP TIME** 40 *Minutes*	**TOTAL TIME** 1 *Hour* 20 *Minutes*	MAKE AHEAD

¼ cup (60 ml)	buttermilk
1 clove	garlic, minced
8 or 9	chicken pieces (I like to use 4 thighs and 4 drumsticks)
1½ cups (375 ml)	dry or fresh whole wheat bread-crumbs (about 6 slices of bread)
2 Tbsp (30 ml)	fresh thyme
1½ tsp (7 ml)	lemon zest
pinch of	salt and pepper

> **TIP** To make your own breadcrumbs, use lightly toasted, not stale, bread. Stale bread equals stale breadcrumbs! Just break up the toasted bread and pulse it in a food processor. Store in an airtight container.

> **GET AHEAD** Save time by completing step 1 the night before or the morning of the meal.

1. Combine the buttermilk and garlic in a shallow pan. Add the chicken pieces, turning to coat thoroughly, then cover with plastic wrap. Place in the fridge to marinate for at least half an hour or overnight. Turn the chicken pieces over at least once while marinating.

2. Preheat the oven to 400°F (200°C).

3. In a bowl, stir together your breadcrumbs, thyme, lemon zest, and salt and pepper. Drain the chicken pieces and dredge them in the breadcrumbs, then arrange on a rack in a roasting pan. Press crumbs onto the chicken if some coating falls off.

4. Bake for 30 to 40 minutes, until the chicken is deeply golden and the meat is cooked through. I always cut into chicken to check it—you don't want to see any red at all.

ZESTY CHICKEN WITH RED BEANS AND RICE

When you accidentally book swimming lessons on the same day your kids have gymnastics—Dear Self, it's called a calendar, try it—you need a dinner like this one waiting for them at the end of the day. It's exactly what a young athlete needs to replenish after lots of action, with lean protein from the chicken and carbs from the beans and rice. Plus, it's really delicious—a big-time favorite in my house. **CM**

MAKES **6** *Servings*	PREP TIME **5** *Minutes*	TOTAL TIME **1** *Hour*	MAKE AHEAD, ACTIVE KIDS

¼ cup (60 ml)	all-purpose flour
4 tsp (20 ml)	chili powder
¼ tsp (1 ml)	salt
¼ tsp (1 ml)	pepper
6	chicken thighs (boneless, skinless or bone-in, with skin)
1 Tbsp (15 ml)	olive oil
2 cloves	garlic, minced
1 can (15 oz/425 g)	red kidney beans, drained and rinsed
1 can (19 oz/540 ml)	diced tomatoes
1 cup (250 ml)	fresh, frozen or drained canned corn
1 cup (250 ml)	brown rice
1 cup (250 ml)	low sodium chicken stock
small handful of	chopped cilantro
1 or 2	limes, quartered

1. Preheat the oven to 350°F (180°C).

2. On a plate, toss together the flour, chili powder, salt and pepper. Dredge the chicken, coating well on all sides.

3. In a Dutch oven or large oven-safe pot, heat the oil over medium-high heat. Working in batches, brown the chicken on both sides but don't cook the meat through, about 3 minutes on each side. Transfer the browned chicken to a clean plate. Drain excess fat from the pot—it's fine if you leave a bit behind for flavor.

4. Turn the heat down to medium-low, add the garlic and allow it to soften up and become fragrant but not turn brown. Now add your beans, tomatoes with their juice, corn, rice and stock. Give everything a nice stir and scrape up anything that is sticking to the bottom. Raise the heat and bring the mixture just to a boil.

5. Place the chicken pieces on top of your tomatoey mixture, put a lid on the whole thing and pop it in the oven for 45 to 50 minutes. Pull out a couple of grains of rice to be sure they're cooked. If your family is game, serve with a sprinkling of cilantro and a squeeze of lime juice.

SLOW COOKER BUTTER CHICKEN

On top of this being an insanely delicious dinner, its genius is you need to do next to no prep before turning on your slow cooker and getting on with your day. No browning chicken at 7 a.m. for me, thanks very much. At dinnertime you'll just need to make some rice to serve this over. Coconut oil in place of butter gives this recipe an even deeper flavor. **CM**

MAKES 6 *Servings*	PREP TIME 10 *Minutes*	TOTAL TIME 6 *Hours* 10 *Minutes*	MAKE AHEAD

2 lb (900 g)	boneless, skinless chicken thighs or breasts, cut into bite-size pieces
1	onion, chopped
3 or 4 cloves	garlic, minced
1 tsp (5 ml)	minced fresh ginger
2/3 cup (150 ml)	tomato paste (or a 5 oz/147 ml tube)
1 heaping Tbsp (about 20 ml)	curry powder or red curry paste
1 can (14 oz/400 ml)	coconut milk
1/2 cup (125 ml)	plain Greek-style yogurt
1/4 cup (60 ml)	milk
2 Tbsp (30 ml)	coconut oil

TIP Swap in butter if you don't have coconut oil.

1. Put everything in the slow cooker and stir it all around. Cover and cook on low for 6 hours. If you won't be home for longer, not to worry, the Butter Chicken will be fine waiting for you in the slow cooker even if it turns off.

2. Serve with a big spoonful of jasmine rice and a sprinkling of chopped cilantro.

BEEF AND MUSHROOM STEW

Taking a few minutes to dredge your meat in seasoned flour will help you get the rich, creamy broth you're looking for with this stew. Whether you're cooking this fresh or reheating the batch you put in the freezer (like a boss), the scent of this dish fills your home with aromatherapy on a cold and wintry night. CM

MAKES **6** *Servings*	PREP TIME **15** *Minutes*	TOTAL TIME **90** *Minutes*	ACTIVE KIDS, MAKE AHEAD

2 Tbsp (30 ml)	all-purpose flour
pinch of	salt and pepper
2 lb (900 g)	stewing beef
2 Tbsp (30 ml)	olive oil
2	onions, diced
3 cloves	garlic, minced
1 lb (450 g)	button or cremini mushrooms, halved or quartered, depending on size
2 sprigs	fresh thyme
⅓ cup (75 ml)	tomato paste
½ cup (125 ml)	white or red wine (optional)
4 cups (1 L)	low-sodium beef stock
2 large	carrots, diced

1. On a plate, toss together the flour, salt and pepper. Dredge the beef, making sure that every surface gets a light coating.

2. In a big pot or Dutch oven, warm the oil over medium heat. Working in batches, brown your meat on all sides, but don't cook it through. Don't over-crowd the pot or you won't get the nice brown crust you're looking to form. Transfer the cooked meat to a clean plate. There will be lots of gunky brown stuff on the bottom of your pot, and that is good.

GET AHEAD Save 10 minutes by prepping your veggies in advance.

3. Add the onions and garlic to the pot and cook, stirring often, for about 3 minutes. Now stir in the mushrooms and thyme. It will take a few moments for the mushrooms to begin to soften. Keep stirring everything around. Now add the tomato paste and stir again so everything gets coated. Let that cook for a couple of minutes.

4. If you're cooking with wine, add it now. It's not necessary but it does add a great flavor (and don't worry—all the alcohol will burn off). Use a wooden spoon to scrape the bottom of the pot to loosen all that caramelized beefy goodness. Add the stock and the beef, bring to a simmer, cover and let simmer for about an hour, until beef is very tender.

5. Stir in the carrots and cook just until they're tender, about 10 more minutes. Remove the thyme sprigs before serving.

HERB SHORT RIBS

Since short ribs can be pricey, we recommend you save this dish for a celebratory occasion. For instance, the intense deliciousness of this dish and its oh-so-fancy presentation over polenta (since it has magical abilities to drink up sauce) makes acing exams feel that much sweeter. **LK**

MAKES 4 *Servings*	**PREP TIME** 25 *Minutes*	**TOTAL TIME** 8 *Hours*	MAKE AHEAD

SHORT RIBS

3 lb (1.3 kg)	flanker-cut short ribs
2 Tbsp (30 ml)	vegetable oil
pinch of	salt and pepper
2	shallots, diced
5 cloves	garlic, minced
2 cups (500 ml)	red wine
1 cup (250 ml)	beef stock
4 sprigs	fresh thyme

POLENTA

2 cups (500 ml)	low-sodium chicken broth
2 cups (500 ml)	water
1 cup (250 ml)	cornmeal
½ cup (125 ml)	grated Parmesan cheese
1 Tbsp (15 ml)	butter
pinch of	salt and pepper

1. Brush each rib all over with oil and generously season all sides with salt and pepper.

2. Heat a large cast-iron skillet over medium-high heat. Add the ribs in one layer; work in batches if you have to in order to not crowd the pan. Sear the ribs for several minutes on each side. Transfer the ribs to a slow cooker.

3. Lower the heat and add the shallots and garlic. Cook, stirring occasionally, until the onions soften, about 5 minutes. Add the red wine and stock and bring to a simmer. Pour the liquid over the ribs in the slow cooker. Place the fresh thyme sprigs on top. Cover and cook on Low for 7 to 8 hours, or until the meat is tender.

4. About 15 minutes before serving, make the polenta. Bring the broth and water to a simmer in a large pot. Gently pour the cornmeal into the bubbling water, whisking constantly. It will thicken quite quickly. Reduce heat to low and cook, stirring constantly, for about 10 minutes. Stir in the Parmesan and butter. Season with salt and pepper.

5. Remove the short ribs from the slow cooker and pull the meat away from the bones. Serve meat over polenta with a spoonful or two of sauce.

TIP You could also serve this with our amazing polenta (recipe on page 148) or over pappardelle.

SLOW COOKER RAGÙ

When Scarlett receives the school's award for "Caring and Kindness" or comes home with a great report card, we head to Nodo, a neighborhood Italian restaurant with traditional mouthwatering dishes, for a celebratory dinner. Scarlett always orders the rigatoni with the slow-cooked ragù. This is my version of that luxurious sauce. I've been privy to the restaurant's recipe, and it's a time-consuming and difficult process, but I think this dish—combining pork and beef—offers the same intense flavor without all the work. It's definitely worthy of an impressive report card. **LK**

MAKES 6 *to* 8 *Servings*	**PREP TIME** 10 *Minutes*	**TOTAL TIME** 8 *Hours* 10 *Minutes*	MAKE AHEAD

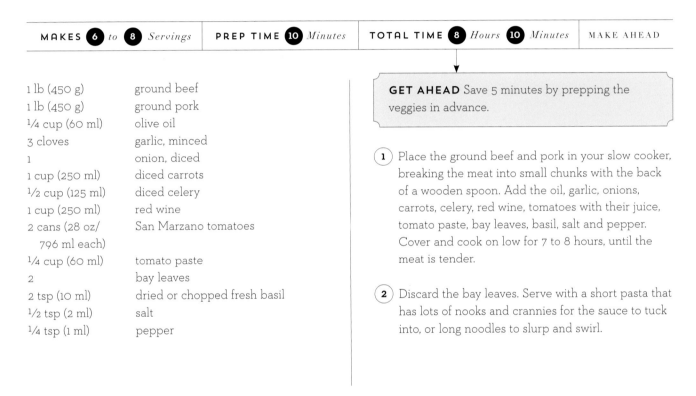

1 lb (450 g)	ground beef
1 lb (450 g)	ground pork
¼ cup (60 ml)	olive oil
3 cloves	garlic, minced
1	onion, diced
1 cup (250 ml)	diced carrots
½ cup (125 ml)	diced celery
1 cup (250 ml)	red wine
2 cans (28 oz/ 796 ml each)	San Marzano tomatoes
¼ cup (60 ml)	tomato paste
2	bay leaves
2 tsp (10 ml)	dried or chopped fresh basil
½ tsp (2 ml)	salt
¼ tsp (1 ml)	pepper

GET AHEAD Save 5 minutes by prepping the veggies in advance.

1. Place the ground beef and pork in your slow cooker, breaking the meat into small chunks with the back of a wooden spoon. Add the oil, garlic, onions, carrots, celery, red wine, tomatoes with their juice, tomato paste, bay leaves, basil, salt and pepper. Cover and cook on low for 7 to 8 hours, until the meat is tender.

2. Discard the bay leaves. Serve with a short pasta that has lots of nooks and crannies for the sauce to tuck into, or long noodles to slurp and swirl.

CHICKPEA AND CAULIFLOWER CURRY WITH BROWN RICE

When life hands you winter, eat this curry. It's hearty, full of fiber and immune-boosting phytonutrients (thank you, chickpeas, tomatoes and cauliflower) and leaves you with leftovers that snuggle sweetly into a thermos. **LK**

MAKES 6 *Servings*	PREP TIME 25 *Minutes*	TOTAL TIME 50 *Minutes*	MAKE AHEAD, VEGETARIAN

2 Tbsp (30 ml)	coconut oil
1 large	onion, finely chopped
2 cloves	garlic, minced
1½ inches (4 cm)	fresh ginger, peeled and minced
2 tsp (10 ml)	ground coriander
2 tsp (10 ml)	ground cumin
1 tsp (5 ml)	ground cinnamon
1 tsp (5 ml)	ground turmeric
1 can (28 oz/796 ml)	diced tomatoes
1 can (15 oz/425 g)	chickpeas, drained and rinsed
1 can (14 oz/400 ml)	coconut milk
1	medium cauliflower, cut into florets
2 tsp (10 ml)	garam masala
	salt and pepper
handful of	chopped cilantro, plus more for garnish

GET AHEAD Save 5 minutes by prepping the onion, garlic and ginger in advance.

1. In a Dutch oven, heat the coconut oil over medium heat. Add the onions, garlic and ginger and cook, stirring often, for 8 to 10 minutes, until softened.

2. Stir in the coriander, cumin, cinnamon and turmeric and cook, stirring, until they are fragrant, about 1 minute. Add the tomatoes with their juice, chickpeas, coconut milk and cauliflower. Increase the heat and bring to a boil, then reduce the heat to low. Cover and simmer for about 15 minutes.

3. Stir in the garam masala and cook, uncovered, for 5 to 10 minutes more, until the sauce thickens slightly. Season with salt and pepper and stir in fresh cilantro. Serve over brown rice and garnish with a bit more cilantro.

TIP Make some mini sliders to use in school lunches.

FALAFEL BURGERS

Rather than place these effortless burgers in our 30-minute dinner section, I've put them here because of two steps in the method that make all the difference to the taste and ease of these patties. First, start with dried beans to yield a burger that isn't super mushy, and second, chill the mix before forming the burgers to make shaping them a lot less messy. If you're going to cut corners to make this dish go from fridge to table fast, you can omit the chilling, but always use dried beans. **LK**

MAKES **6** *to* **8** *Burgers*		**PREP TIME** **1** *Hour* **10** *Minutes*		

TOTAL TIME *Overnight Plus* **1** *Hour* **16** *Minutes* | MAKE AHEAD, VEGETARIAN

GET AHEAD Save 5 minutes by prepping your onions, garlic and ginger in advance.

2 cups (500 ml)	dried chickpeas
1	small white onion, roughly chopped
2 cloves	garlic, chopped
¼ cup (60 ml)	chopped flat-leaf or curly parsley
2 Tbsp (30 ml)	all-purpose flour
1½ tsp (7 ml)	salt
2 tsp (10 ml)	ground cumin
1 tsp (5 ml)	ground coriander
½ tsp (2 ml)	chili powder
2 Tbsp (30 ml)	grapeseed oil
for serving:	toasted pita bread, sliced cucumber, tahini sauce

1. The night before, place chickpeas in a large bowl and cover with cold water. In the morning, drain, rinse and pat the beans dry and store in the refrigerator until you're ready to use them.

2. Pour the chickpeas into a food processor, then add the onions, garlic, parsley, flour, salt, cumin, coriander and chili powder. Process until the mixture is a coarse meal, scraping down the sides occasionally. Scrape the mixture into a bowl, cover and refrigerate for an hour. (You can skip this step but the patties will be stickier to work with.)

3. Shape the mixture into 6 to 8 patties with damp hands.

4. Warm the oil in a large nonstick skillet over medium heat. Add the burgers and cook until lightly golden brown on the bottom, about 3 minutes. Flip and cook until golden brown, another 3 minutes. Drain on paper towels. Serve in toasted pitas with sliced cucumber and tahini sauce.

TIP This recipe yields enough sauce to complete this dish and have extra to store in an airtight container in the refrigerator or freezer for another meal. God bless the double batch.

BAKED RIGATONI WITH SPINACH AND RICOTTA

There is no other dish like a baked pasta—filling a home with that aroma of bursting tomatoes and melting cheese—that reminds me so much of my mother. I guess my need to make one a week is something I unknowingly inherited from her. It's just something that happens to you when you become a parent: you end up saying and doing the things you swore you'd never say and do. However, when it comes to watching my family excitedly gather around the table for an oozing casserole of pasta, I feel like how my mother must feel—like she got it right. **LK**

MAKES **6** *Servings*	PREP TIME **30** *Minutes*	TOTAL TIME **1** *Hour*	MAKE AHEAD, VEGETARIAN

TOMATO SAUCE

4 tsp (20 ml)	olive oil
2	yellow onions, diced
4 cloves	garlic, minced
2 cans	whole San Marzano tomatoes (28 oz/796 ml each)
2 Tbsp (30 ml)	tomato paste
3 Tbsp (45 ml)	dried basil
½ tsp (2 ml)	salt
½ tsp (2 ml)	pepper
2 Tbsp (30 ml)	chopped fresh parsley
½ tsp (2 ml)	sugar (optional)

CASSEROLE

1 lb (450 g)	rigatoni
1 package	fresh or frozen spinach, thawed (10 oz/284 g)
2 cups (500 ml)	ricotta cheese
¼ cup (60 ml)	grated Parmesan cheese
½ tsp (2 ml)	salt
1 cup (250 ml)	grated Fontina cheese, divided
½ cup (125 ml)	grated mozzarella cheese

1. For the sauce, in a large saucepan over medium heat, warm the oil. Add the onions and garlic and cook, stirring often, for 5 minutes or until the onions are softened. Add the tomatoes with their juice, breaking tomatoes up with the back of a spoon. Stir in the tomato paste, basil, salt and pepper. Bring to a boil, reduce heat and simmer, uncovered, for about 20 minutes. Stir in the parsley. If the sauce tastes too acidic, you can add ½ tsp (2 ml) sugar. Season with additional salt and pepper if necessary. If you prefer a smooth sauce, process it in batches in a food processor.

2. Preheat the oven to 350°F (180°C).

3. In a large pot of salted water, cook the rigatoni halfway, about 6 minutes. Drain. Put the pasta back into the pot and toss with a ladle or two of your sauce. Set aside.

4. Meanwhile, if using frozen, thaw and then remove as much water as possible from the spinach by squeezing it with your hands. In a food processor, whiz the ricotta, Parmesan and salt. Stir in the spinach and half of the Fontina. Stir the ricotta mixture into the pasta.

5. Spread an even layer of tomato sauce across the bottom of a 13- by 9-inch (3 L) baking dish. Spread the pasta mixture evenly in the dish. Spoon a bit more sauce over the top, then sprinkle with the remaining Fontina as well as the mozzarella. Bake until bubbling and the cheese has browned, 15 to 20 minutes. Allow the casserole to rest for 10 minutes before serving.

LENTIL CHILI

This wholesome vegetarian chili is the epitome of Sunday-afternoon cooking. Very little prep is involved, and the chili requires almost no attention as it simmers away. You can absolutely make this while overseeing a ten-page social studies project that was just now discovered at the bottom of somebody's backpack. Ahem. Get this chili in the freezer for later in the week, or have it for dinner tonight and put the leftovers in a thermos to go to school tomorrow (along with your—I mean somebody's—dazzling report). **CM**

MAKES ❽ *Servings*	**PREP TIME** ❺ *Minutes*	**TOTAL TIME** ㉟ *Minutes*	MAKE AHEAD, VEGETARIAN

2 Tbsp (30 ml)	olive oil
1	onion, diced
4 cloves	garlic, minced
2 Tbsp (30 ml)	chili powder
1 tsp (5 ml)	ground cumin
½ cup (125 ml)	brown or green lentils
2	bay leaves
2 cups (500 ml)	water
1 can (19 oz/540 ml)	white navy beans, drained and rinsed
1 can (19 oz/540 ml)	black beans, drained and rinsed
1 can (28 oz/796 ml)	whole tomatoes
1 cup (250 ml)	vegetable stock
	salt and pepper
Toppings:	grated cheddar cheese, chopped cilantro, salsa, sour cream or Greek yogurt

TIP Green and brown lentils hold their shape better than red lentils.

1. In a large pot or Dutch oven, warm the oil over medium heat. Add the onions and garlic and push them around every once in a while until they soften, about 3 minutes. Add the chili powder and cumin, give everything a stir and allow the spices to cook for a minute or two.

2. Add the lentils, bay leaves and water. Bring to a gentle boil and let simmer for 5 minutes.

3. Add the beans, the tomatoes with their juice and the stock. Let it bubble away gently for 20 minutes. Remove the bay leaves. Season with salt and pepper if needed. Serve the chili over rice or with a nice piece of cornbread. But do not scrimp on the toppings—it's not chili to me without a good sprinkling of cheese and a dollop of sour cream or Greek yogurt.

CLASSIC TUNA CASSEROLE

Having a good old-fashioned tuna casserole in the freezer can be your secret superpower. Knowing it's waiting there, ready to feed swimming-lesson-hungry kids (is there another activity that creates that level of hunger?) takes the edge off having to reassure them about three hundred times on the drive home that you're going to feed them soon. **CM**

MAKES **6** *Servings*	PREP TIME **5** *Minutes*	TOTAL TIME **35** *Minutes*	MAKE AHEAD

1 lb (450 g)	short whole wheat pasta such as penne
1 Tbsp (15 ml)	olive oil
3 cups (750 ml)	cremini mushrooms, thinly sliced
1	leek, thinly sliced
3 Tbsp (45 ml)	all-purpose flour
2 cups (500 ml)	milk
1 Tbsp (15 ml)	Dijon mustard
	salt and pepper
3 cans (7 oz/198 g each)	tuna packed in oil, drained
1 cup (250 ml)	frozen peas
1 Tbsp (15 ml)	dried thyme
1½ cups (375 ml)	grated gruyère cheese

GET AHEAD Save 5 minutes by prepping your veggies in advance.

1. Bring a large pot of salted water to a boil. Add pasta and cook until al dente and no more, about 8 minutes. Drain.

2. Meanwhile, in a large skillet, warm the oil over medium heat. Add the mushrooms and leeks and cook, stirring occasionally, until they begin to soften, about 5 minutes.

3. Sprinkle flour over the mushroom mixture and stir. Cook for about 1 minute. Whisk in milk and allow the sauce to thicken, 3 to 5 minutes. If the sauce doesn't thicken, inch up the heat just a bit.

4. Stir in the mustard and season with salt and pepper. Stir in the tuna, frozen peas and thyme. Add the drained pasta and stir again. Pour the mixture into 13-inch by 9-inch (3 L) casserole dish.

5. Preheat the broiler to low with a rack in the upper third. Sprinkle the cheese over the casserole and broil for 3 to 5 minutes, until the cheese bubbles and turns brown.

TIP If you're going to make this ahead, do everything except broiling the cheese before placing it in the freezer. Loosely cover the frozen casserole with foil and reheat in a 350°F (180°C) oven for about 45 minutes. Check that it's warm in the center, then remove the foil and broil the cheese.

LEFTOVER MAKEOVERS

Remember when you were single and you turned your nose up at leftovers? Wasn't that cute? Now that you're an adult whom others—children, mainly—rely on for sustenance, you've come to embrace those leftovers like old friends. Haven't you?! You don't need to straight up reheat last night's dinner, and there's more to leftovers than a sandwich. (Although, we love a good sandwich). Let this easy guide inspire you to take your leftovers and Houdini them into what feels like a shiny new dish showing everyone you're the boss. But, really: As if they didn't already know that.

AUDIT YOUR LEFTOVERS. Choose from what you have in your fridge and freezer and decide what makes sense together. For instance, you may not want to pair your leftover tomato sauce from one night with another night's chili spiced beef. In that case, decide on one and move forward.

SELECT A DISH. Pick a meal that makes sense for your leftovers and be sure to take into account the extras you'll need. Don't forget to consider other fresh ingredients in your fridge or pantry to fill out your new leftover-based recipe. This is a great time to use the rest of those celery stalks or the other half of the onion from Tuesday night's chili.

FRITTATA

YOUR LEFTOVERS: 1 cup (250 ml) of any combination of cooked protein or vegetables (or make up the difference with lightly sautéed vegetables).

EXTRAS YOU NEED: 8 eggs; ⅓ cup (75 ml) milk; 1 Tbsp (15 ml) Dijon mustard; ½ cup (125 ml) grated cheese; herbs.

(1) Preheat oven to 350°F (180°C).

(2) Dice your leftovers into similar-size pieces.

(3) In a large bowl, whisk together eggs, milk and mustard until well combined. Season with salt and pepper.

(4) Add a splash of oil to a large, oven-proof skillet. Cook any fresh ingredients first and then add leftovers to warm.

(5) Pour in your egg mixture. Sprinkle cheese over top and any herbs you may be adding. Allow the eggs to just begin to set, about 2 or 3 minutes, then carefully place the skillet in the oven and bake for 10 to 15 minutes. Watch it at the end—you want to make sure the egg has set and cheese has melted. If you'd like it a little golden brown, turn the oven to broil for 1 minute.

(6) Remove from the oven and allow to cool slightly before cutting into wedges.

GRAIN BOWL

MAKES **4** *Bowls*

YOUR LEFTOVERS: 2 cups (500 ml) any combination of cooked proteins and vegetables (or make up the difference with lightly sautéed vegetables).

EXTRAS YOU NEED: 4 servings of grain (rice, couscous, quinoa or barley); chopped fresh vegetables (carrot, peppers and cucumber); protein, legumes or healthy fats like avocado, egg or beans; cheese; dressing.

(1) Prepare your grain according to package instructions, and divide it amongst the bowls.

(2) Reheat the leftovers and add to the bowls of grain.

(3) Add the chopped vegetables and the protein, legumes or healthy fats, if using.

(4) Top with cheese and fresh herbs, and maybe a dressing, if desired.

 **WATCH** Don't forget to check out our exclusive video with step-by-step instructions on how to make a grain bowl and other grain bowl inspiration. Find it on sweetpotatochronicles.com.

QUESADILLAS

MAKES **2** *Quesadillas*

YOUR LEFTOVERS: 2 cups (500 ml) any combination of cooked proteins and vegetables (or make up the difference with lightly sautéed vegetables).

EXTRAS YOU NEED: 4 tortillas; 1 cup (250 ml) grated cheese.

(1) Take your leftovers and dice them up into similar-size pieces and then warm them in a microwave or skillet.

(2) Heat up a tiny bit of oil in a large skillet over medium heat.

(3) Place one tortilla in the skillet and spread 1 cup (250 ml) of leftovers across it, then sprinkle ½ cup (125 ml) cheese over top. Place another tortilla on top.

(4) Press down firmly with a plate or the back of a spatula. Cook for 5 minutes until the underside of the tortilla is golden brown.

(5) Use a spatula under the quesadilla and your hand on top and quickly flip it over.

(6) Cook for another 5 minutes, until brown on the other side. Repeat process for the second quesadilla.

(7) Serve with sour cream or yogurt, salsa and sliced avocado or guacamole.

 WATCH See our exclusive video for turning leftovers into new and delicious dinners on our website.

SAVORY BREAD PUDDING

MAKES **4** *Servings*

YOUR LEFTOVERS: 1 cup (250 ml) any combination of cooked proteins and vegetables (or make up the difference with lightly sautéed vegetables).

EXTRAS YOU NEED: 2 cups (500 ml) crusty bread, cut into 1-inch (2.5 cm) cubes; ½ cup (125 ml) grated gruyere cheese; 6 eggs; ¼ cup (60 ml) milk; herbs.

1. Preheat the oven to 400°F (200°C).

2. Grease a 9-inch (23 cm) square casserole dish.

3. Dice leftovers into similar-size pieces.

4. In a large mixing bowl, toss the bread, leftovers and cheese.

5. In a separate bowl, whisk the eggs and milk. Add them to the bread mixture and stir. Sprinkle in an herb—it's best to use one that you used in the leftovers.

6. Pour the mixture into the prepared dish. Bake in the oven and cook until golden brown, about 25 minutes, or until egg is set.

"I don't always need my snacks
at school but I always feel like
I need dessert."

SCARLETT, AGE 10

"I don't mind
once-a-week
dessert
because
I'm healthy."

JULIAN, AGE 7

"When I get home from school
I like crackers."

ESME, AGE 10

Snacks
and Treats

SMARTEN UP THOSE SNACKS

Of all the challenges that come with feeding kids, snacks strike me as the cruelest. Just when you've figured out a plan for breakfast, lunch and dinner and you're feeling like a rock star, along comes a hungry kid looking for a snack to cut you down to mortal size. In the preschool years I used to joke that park snacks were in my parenting blind spot. But it doesn't take long to realize the important place that snacks hold in a kid's daily nutrition. And as kids get bigger and busier with activities, snacks are downright essential to keeping them happy and healthy. **CM**

1 FILL IN NUTRITIONAL BLANKS. Think of snacks as another chance to hit the five to six servings of fruits and vegetables or the four to six grain servings school-aged kids should be consuming. Using snacks to hit those serving goals also takes some pressure off mealtimes, and who wouldn't want that?

2 BALANCE BLOOD SUGAR. A snack keeps your kids going. Maintaining energy via level blood sugar is critical to their ability to focus and learn in school. It also makes them happier and calmer, which is good for them and for everyone around them.

3 SELECT THE RIGHT SNACK. Those little bites really count, but only when you make them count. There are lots of store-bought nibbles out there that will fill up your kids, but you want to achieve a balance between protein and complex carbohydrates and avoid too much sugar. There's nothing wrong with supplementing homemade snacks with store-bought ones—just be mindful of what's on the ingredient label. Apple slices with store-bought whole grain crackers and peanut butter makes a great combo. A store-bought granola bar packed with sugar, not so much.

4 WHY THE TREATS? So, big talk. What, then, are treats doing in this book? Listen, there was a debate. A debate between us authors, a debate among our community on Facebook and Instagram, where we posed the question. And here's where we landed: This book is all about your whole life during the school year, which includes Friday nights, celebrations for good report cards, bake sales and potluck dinners for the soccer team. The school year just has to include some treats.

TIP See recipe for Lemon Cardamom Apple Cake (left) on page 202.

NUT-FREE ENERGY BITES

These bite-size energy bombs are easy to whip together and even easier to pack for soccer or dance class. They're not crumbly the way granola bars can be, so they won't make a mess in the car. (Not that I ever break the no-food-in-the-car rule, obvs.) **CM**

MAKES **20** to **24** Balls	PREP TIME **5** Minutes

TOTAL TIME **45** Minutes

MAKE AHEAD, VEGETARIAN, PORTABLE

1 cup (250 ml)	oats
2/3 cup (150 ml)	unsweetened shredded coconut
1 Tbsp (15 ml)	chia seeds
1/2 cup (125 ml)	ground flax
1/2 cup (125 ml)	chocolate chips
1/2 cup (125 ml)	sunflower butter
1/3 cup (75 ml)	maple syrup
1 tsp (5 ml)	vanilla extract

(1) In a large bowl, mix all ingredients until well combined. Cover and refrigerate for at least half an hour.

(2) Once your dough is chilled, roll into 1-inch (2.5 cm) balls. Store in an airtight container in the fridge for up to 1 week.

SCHOOL-SAFE CHOCOLATE SNACK BALLS

Snacks for school used to haunt me because the tides changed so quickly with Scarlett and her need for noshies—some weeks I couldn't pack enough and other times they became a well-decayed science project in her book bag. It wasn't just the level of her appetite but what she was craving. I made these balls using some of her favorite flavors—chocolate, coconut, apricots—so they always seem to fit the bill. And she can safely trade them with friends if they're suddenly not meeting her fancy. Let's be honest, we know trades happen. **LK**

MAKES About **12** Balls

PREP TIME **15** Minutes

TOTAL TIME **1** Hour **15** Minutes

MAKE AHEAD, VEGETARIAN, PORTABLE

1 cup (250 ml)	dried apricots
1/2 cup (125 ml)	unsweetened shredded coconut, divided
1/4 cup (60 ml)	raw pumpkin seeds
1/4 cup (60 ml)	raw and unsalted sunflower seeds
1/4 cup (60 ml)	cocoa powder
1 Tbsp (15 ml)	honey
1 tsp (5 ml)	coconut oil, melted

(1) Line a baking sheet with parchment paper. In a food processor, pulse the dried apricots, 1/4 cup (60 ml) of the coconut, pumpkin seeds, sunflower seeds and cocoa until the mixture is crumbly. Add the honey and coconut oil and process again until a sticky, uniform dough is created.

(2) Place the remaining coconut on a plate. Scoop a heaping tablespoon of the dough and roll into a ball with wet hands. Roll in coconut and place on the baking sheet; continue with the remaining dough. Refrigerate for at least 1 hour. Store in an airtight container in the refrigerator for up to 1 week.

An
all-star snack
is the best way
to celebrate
making the
basketball team—
finally.

MORNING GLORY MUFFINS

These muffins are packed with fruit and veggies, but they don't feel like one of those compromise snacks kids will eat when they can tell you're not going to hand over the last of the Halloween candy, you know? These are tender and sweet, with great texture. **CM**

| MAKES **12** *Muffins* | PREP TIME **15** *Minutes* | TOTAL TIME **40** *Minutes* | MAKE AHEAD, VEGETARIAN |

2 cups (500 ml)	grated peeled carrots
1 cup (250 ml)	grated peeled apple
1 cup (250 ml)	all-purpose flour
1 cup (250 ml)	whole wheat flour
¾ cup (175 ml)	sugar
¼ cup (60 ml)	ground flax
1½ tsp (7 ml)	baking powder
¾ tsp (4 ml)	baking soda
1 tsp (5 ml)	ground cinnamon
½ tsp (2 ml)	salt
1 cup (250 ml)	unsweetened shredded coconut
½ cup (125 ml)	chopped pecans (or walnuts or almonds or leave out altogether)
½ cup (125 ml)	raisins
3	eggs
¾ cup (175 ml)	vegetable oil or melted coconut oil
1 tsp (5 ml)	vanilla extract

1. Preheat the oven to 350°F (180°C). Grease a 12-cup muffin tin or line with paper liners.

2. In a bowl, toss together the grated carrots and apple. Set aside.

3. In a large bowl, whisk together the all-purpose flour, whole wheat flour, sugar, flax, baking powder, baking soda, cinnamon and salt. Add the coconut, nuts and raisins and toss well. (Tossing the nuts and raisins with the flour mixture stops them from sinking to the bottom of the muffins.)

4. In a small bowl, whisk together the eggs, oil and vanilla. Add the wet ingredients to the dry ingredients and stir until just combined. Stir in the grated carrots and apple.

5. Spoon the batter into the muffin cups. Bake for 20 to 25 minutes, until a toothpick comes out clean. Turn out onto a rack to cool completely. Store in an airtight container in a cool spot for up to 5 days or in the freezer for up to 3 months.

BANANA CHOCOLATE QUINOA BARS

Granola bars are an obvious addition to a packed lunch—they're portable, energy-boosting and kid-approved. But so many store-bought bars are little more than candy. These not-too-sweet bars are winners when it comes to taste *and* nutrition. **CM**

MAKES **18** *Bars*	PREP TIME **10** *Minutes*	TOTAL TIME **50** *Minutes*	MAKE AHEAD, VEGETARIAN

3	super-ripe bananas
3 Tbsp (45 ml)	sunflower butter
¼ cup (60 ml)	brown rice syrup or corn syrup
2 Tbsp (30 ml)	maple syrup
1 Tbsp (15 ml)	coconut oil
1 tsp (5 ml)	ground cinnamon
½ tsp (2 ml)	salt
3 cups (750 ml)	oats
1 cup (250 ml)	quinoa
½ cup (125 ml)	chocolate chips (I use half choc chips and half cacao nibs)

OPTIONAL DRIZZLE

¼ cup (60 ml)	chocolate chips
1 Tbsp (15 ml)	coconut oil

> **TIP** Sub in almond or peanut butter if these beauties aren't heading to school.

1. Preheat the oven to 350°F (180°C). Line a 13- by 9-inch (3 L) baking pan with parchment paper, leaving some overhang on each long side to help you lift your bars out later.

2. In a stand mixer fitted with the paddle or with an electric mixer, beat the bananas, sunflower butter, brown rice syrup, maple syrup, coconut oil, cinnamon and salt until it's a nice creamy consistency.

3. In a large bowl, toss together the oats, quinoa and chocolate chips. Shake the dry ingredients into the bowl of banana mixture. Stir with the mixer until everything is completely combined. You may need to stop to scrape down the edges of the bowl. Turn everything out of the bowl and into the baking pan. Spread the batter so it goes right to the edges of the pan. Smooth the top using a spatula.

4. Bake for 40 to 45 minutes, until golden. Allow it to cool completely before applying the drizzle.

5. In a small saucepan, heat the remaining chocolate chips and coconut oil over very low heat, stirring now and then, until they melt. Pop the sauce in the fridge for a moment to firm slightly. Use a small spoon or spatula to drizzle chocolate over your bars. Lift the bars from the pan and cut into 18 pieces. Store in an airtight container in a cool spot for up to 1 week. Just before packing them into a lunch, wrap them in plastic wrap or parchment paper to keep the chocolate from coming off.

PUMPKIN CORNBREAD

Heaven, people. This cornbread is heaven. Aside from being a skillet full of buttery and crumbly goodness, it also lays claim to having the health benefits of pumpkin, an antioxidant dynamo. I have yet to meet the kid who can pass on this snack. If you meet them, just smother a piece of this with cinnamon butter and you'll hook them too. **LK**

| MAKES **8** *Servings* | PREP TIME **10** *Minutes* | TOTAL TIME **35** *Minutes* | VEGETARIAN |

½ cup (125 ml)	butter (1 stick)
1 cup (250 ml)	corn flour
¾ cup (175 ml)	all-purpose flour
¼ cup (60 ml)	finely ground cornmeal
¼ cup (60 ml)	sugar
2 tsp (10 ml)	baking powder
½ tsp (2 ml)	baking soda
¼ tsp (1 ml)	ground cinnamon
pinch of	freshly grated nutmeg
1 tsp (5 ml)	salt
1	egg, lightly beaten
1 cup (250 ml)	buttermilk
⅓ cup (75 ml)	milk
¼ cup (60 ml)	pumpkin purée

1. Preheat the oven to 400°F (200°C). Melt the butter in a 9-inch (23 cm) cast-iron skillet in the preheating oven, then set aside.

2. In a large bowl, whisk together the corn flour, all-purpose flour, cornmeal, sugar, baking powder, baking soda, cinnamon, nutmeg and salt. In a separate bowl, whisk the egg, then whisk in the buttermilk, milk and pumpkin purée. Slowly add the wet ingredients to the dry, stirring until well combined. Add almost all the melted butter from the skillet, leaving enough to coat the skillet, and then stir to combine.

3. Pour the batter into the skillet and bake until lightly browned, about 15 to 20 minutes. Allow to cool a bit before serving. Store in an airtight container in the refrigerator for up to a week if you can keep it that long.

TIP If you want a traditional cornbread to make your Tex-Mex supper look like it belongs on a ranch, you can simply omit the pumpkin and spices.

HAWAIIAN PIZZA MUFFINS

These muffins were given a rigorous taste-testing from inspectors 11, 12 and 13. In other words, Scarlett and her two best buds, Sam and Caroline (some mighty harsh food critics), wouldn't give these muffins the after-school A-okay until they reached the perfect balance of pizza taste vs. pillowy satisfaction. **LK**

MAKES **12** *Muffins*	PREP TIME **15** *Minutes*	TOTAL TIME **35** *Minutes*	MAKE AHEAD

2 cups (500 ml)	spelt flour
2 Tbsp (30 ml)	sugar
2 tsp (10 ml)	baking powder
½ tsp (2 ml)	dried oregano
½ tsp (2 ml)	garlic powder
¼ tsp (1 ml)	salt
2	eggs
¾ cup (175 ml)	milk
½ cup (125 ml)	vegetable oil
¾ cup (175 ml)	diced ham
¾ cup (175 ml)	grated mozzarella cheese, plus more for topping
¼ cup (60 ml)	diced pineapple
1 Tbsp (15 ml)	chopped fresh basil
¼ cup (60 ml)	pizza sauce

1. Preheat the oven to 350°F (180°C). Line a 12-cup muffin tin with paper liners.

2. In a medium bowl, whisk together the flour, sugar, baking powder, oregano, garlic powder and salt. In a large bowl, whisk the eggs, then whisk in the milk and oil until smooth. Add the flour mixture and stir just until well combined. Stir in the ham, cheese, pineapple and basil.

3. Spoon the batter evenly into the muffin liners. Spoon 1 tsp (5 ml) pizza sauce over each muffin, and then sprinkle with additional mozzarella. Bake for 20 minutes, or until golden brown and a toothpick inserted into a muffin comes out clean. Turn out onto a rack to cool. Store in the refrigerator in an airtight container or bag for up to one week.

TRAIL MIXES

Our love affair with trail mix began with gorp (good old raisins and peanuts). It was as essential to a late-'70s school lunch as Wagon Wheels and a thermos of Tang. While there's nothing wrong with the classics, we've evolved the romance to some more inventive combinations. Whether you're sprinkling them over a breakfast yogurt parfait or just grabbing handfuls out of a mason jar, we love the chewy, crunchy sweet-and-saltiness of these mixes. Whether you choose to use roasted, raw, salted or unsalted nuts is entirely up to you (why not mix it up?). We also love the ease of tossing the ingredients into a mason jar and asking a kid to give it all a shake.

MAKES 2 to 2½ *Cups (500 to 625 ml)*	TOTAL TIME 5 *Minutes*	FAST, MAKE AHEAD, VEGETARIAN

MONKEY MUNCH

½ cup (125 ml)	dried banana chips
½ cup (125 ml)	unsalted roasted peanuts
½ cup (125 ml)	unsweetened shredded coconut or unsweetened coconut flakes
½ cup (125 ml)	chocolate chips
¼ tsp (1 ml)	salt

TROPICAL PUNCH

½ cup (125 ml)	unsweetened coconut flakes
½ cup (125 ml)	dried banana chips
½ cup (125 ml)	cashews
½ cup (125 ml)	macadamia nuts
¼ cup (60 ml)	dried mango, diced

POWER PACK

½ cup (125 ml)	dried blueberries
½ cup (125 ml)	pumpkin seeds
½ cup (125 ml)	almonds
¼ cup (60 ml)	dark chocolate chunks or chips
¼ cup (60 ml)	goji berries

SCHOOL-SAFE SUPER MIX

1 cup (250 ml)	crushed pretzels
½ cup (125 ml)	raw pumpkin seeds
½ cup (125 ml)	golden raisins
¼ cup (60 ml)	shelled sunflower seeds
¼ cup (60 ml)	mini chocolate chips
¼ tsp (1 ml)	ground cinnamon
pinch of	freshly grated nutmeg

EDAMAME GUACAMOLE

(page 184)

BEET HUMMUS

(page 184)

FRUIT SALSA
(page 185)

AVOCADO HUMMUS
(page 185)

ADDICTIVE DIPS

If the book bag is chucked at your feet and your kid instantly breaks into tears because So-and-So is their partner for their stupid science project, then you know it's time for an after-school snack. We've all been on the receiving end of a kid blind with hunger and tired from a long day, so, as a lifesaving measure (theirs), have some nibbles ready. We love a simple dip with veggies, pita chips or crackers. And because being on your toes matters at this slippery time of day, avoid the "not that again" groan with these easy twists on dipping classics. But for heaven's sake, little people, wash your hands first!

EDAMAME GUACAMOLE

MAKES **3** *Cups (750 ml)*

PREP TIME **1** *Hour* **15** *Minutes*

FAST, MAKE AHEAD, VEGETARIAN

2	avocados
1	lime, juiced
1 cup (250 ml)	shelled edamame, cooked and mashed
½ medium	onion, diced
1 Tbsp (15 ml)	chopped cilantro
½ tsp (2 ml)	salt

1. In a medium bowl, roughly mash the avocados with a fork. Mix in the lime juice and edamame. Then stir in the onion, cilantro and salt. Taste and add more salt or cilantro, depending on personal preference.

2. Cover with plastic wrap, pressing down against the guacamole, and refrigerate for an hour.

BEET HUMMUS

MAKES **3** *Cups (750 ml)* | **TOTAL TIME** **25** *Minutes*

MAKE AHEAD, ACTIVE KIDS

GET AHEAD Save 20 minutes by purchasing precooked beets.

2 or 3	medium beets
1 can (15 oz/425 g)	chickpeas, drained and rinsed
¼ cup (60 ml)	lemon juice
4 tsp (20 ml)	tahini
1 tsp (5 ml)	ground cumin
1 tsp (5 ml)	salt

1. You can either roast the beets by wrapping them in foil and placing them in a 350°F (180°C) oven for 45 minutes to an hour, or boil for about 20 minutes. Either way, the beets are cooked when a fork slides easily into the center. Rinse them under cool water until you can handle them. Slip off the skins, trim the ends and roughly chop the beets.

2. In a food processor or blender, process all the ingredients together for at least 2 minutes, or until the hummus is very creamy. You'll need to stop once or twice to scrape down the sides of the blender and stir the ingredients to make sure they all get combined well. Taste and adjust seasoning. Store in an airtight container in the fridge for up to 1 week.

FRUIT SALSA

| MAKES **1** *Cup (250 ml)* | TOTAL TIME **15** *Minutes* |

MAKE AHEAD, VEGETARIAN

4 or 5	strawberries, finely diced
½	English cucumber, peeled and finely diced
½	jalapeño pepper, seeded and minced (optional)
handful of	cilantro leaves
2 Tbsp (30 ml)	lime juice
pinch of	salt and pepper

1. Toss together all the ingredients and taste to check seasoning.

AVOCADO HUMMUS

| MAKES **3** *Cups (750 ml)* | TOTAL TIME **10** *Minutes* |

FAST, MAKE AHEAD, VEGETARIAN

1 can (15 oz/425 g)	chickpeas, drained and rinsed
1 clove	garlic
3 Tbsp (45 ml)	olive oil
3 Tbsp (45 ml)	lime juice
4 tsp (20 ml)	tahini
2	avocados
⅛ tsp (0.5 ml)	ground cumin
pinch of	salt and pepper

1. In a food processor, pulse the chickpeas, garlic, oil, lime juice and tahini until smooth, at least 2 minutes.

2. Scoop the avocado flesh into the food processor. Give it another good mix until your hummus changes from beige to pale green. Add the cumin and salt and pepper to taste. Store in an airtight container in the fridge for up to a week.

SALTED CHOCOLATE POPCORN

Whether it's Friday night or you've got a pack of post-sport hungry mouths, this sweet and savory popcorn mix is a hard act to follow when it comes to snacks. Sorry, greasy potato chips, you just got schooled on tasty. **LK**

MAKES **8** *Cups (2 L)*	PREP TIME **5** *Minutes*	TOTAL TIME **1** *Hour* **30** *Minutes*	MAKE AHEAD, VEGETARIAN

3 Tbsp (45 ml)	coconut oil
1/3 cup (75 ml)	popping corn
1 cup (250 ml)	dark chocolate chips
3 Tbsp (45 ml)	unsalted butter
1½ cups (375 ml)	roughly chopped pretzels
¼ cup (60 ml)	slivered almonds
¼ cup (60 ml)	golden raisins
1 tsp (5 ml)	sea salt

1. Line a baking sheet with parchment paper. In a large saucepan, heat the oil over medium-high heat. Drop in 3 kernels of corn and cover. When you hear the corn pop, add the rest of the corn, cover and remove from the heat for 30 seconds. Place back on the heat and jiggle the pot continuously while the corn pops. When the popping slows nearly to a stop, pour the popcorn into a large bowl.

2. Place the chocolate chips and butter in a heatproof bowl. Fill a saucepan about a quarter full with hot water, sit the bowl over the pan (make sure it's resting on the rim, not touching the water) and place over low heat. Stir occasionally until the butter and chocolate have melted. Pour half the chocolate over the popcorn. Stir to coat.

3. Add 1 cup (250 ml) pretzels, almonds and raisins, then stir. Pour the last of the chocolate over the mix and stir again.

4. Spread the popcorn on the baking sheet and sprinkle with remaining pretzels and salt. Let sit at room temperature until the chocolate has hardened, about 1 hour. Store in an airtight container for up to 3 days, if you can make it last that long.

MINTY SWEET PEA DEVILED EGGS

Come on, admit it. You know you've loved deviled eggs ever since you were a kid. And it's exactly why you should give them to your kids. They look so cheery on a plate, and the velvety yolks are always so appealing against the snap of the whites. However, these aren't your mother's devils. The peas give this retro snack a modern spin. **LK**

MAKES **12** *Deviled Eggs*	PREP TIME **5** *Minutes*	TOTAL TIME **60** *Minutes*	VEGETARIAN

1 tsp (5 ml)   white vinegar
6   eggs
½ cup (125 ml)   frozen peas, cooked
¾ cup (175 ml)   Vegenaise or mayonnaise
1 tsp (5 ml)   olive oil
2 tsp (10 ml)   chopped fresh mint, plus more for garnish
   salt and pepper

1. Fill a large saucepan with water and stir in the vinegar. Gently add the eggs. Be sure the eggs are covered with at least an inch (2.5 cm) of water. Cover, bring to a boil over high heat, stirring gently, then remove from the heat and let stand for 12 minutes. Drain the eggs and place them in a bowl of cold water to chill.

2. Peel the eggs and cut them in half lengthwise. Scoop the yolks into a small bowl. Arrange the whites on a serving plate. Cover and set aside.

3. In a food processor, pulse the yolks, peas, Vegenaise, oil and mint until smooth. Add salt and pepper to taste.

4. Place a resealable plastic bag in a large measuring cup, turning the sides of the bag down around the outside of the cup. Scrape the yolk mixture into the bag. Remove the bag from the measuring cup and seal. Snip off one corner of the bag and pipe the yolk mixture into the whites.

5. Chill in the refrigerator for 30 minutes. Serve with a sprinkling of chopped mint. Store leftovers in an airtight container in the refrigerator for up to 3 days.

TIP Aunt Cathryn made me promise to use all-purpose flour in this recipe, but—don't tell her—I use spelt. Feel free to do what she says. She'll like you better.

AUNT CATHRYN'S PECAN BREAD

My aunt is one of those women you hope to be like when you grow up. (Don't you still aspire to grow up to something? I do.) She's so successful and fiercely passionate about everything in her life—family, work and even baking. Her baking prowess is the stuff of legends in our family—forty-five homemade pies at one Thanksgiving, dozens of holiday cookie tins knocked off in a day. So it was a pretty big deal that I got her to share a recipe that is her personal favorite. She describes this subtly sweet bread that she makes for herself every week as "hard to kill." In other words, you can't mess it up and you can use it for everything—spread with jam for a snack, toasted for breakfast or as the base of sandwiches. It can basically handle anything. Just like my aunt. **LK**

| MAKES **1** *Loaf* | PREP TIME **10** *Minutes* | TOTAL TIME **50** *Minutes* | MAKE AHEAD, VEGETARIAN |

3½ cups (875 ml)	spelt flour
1 tsp (5 ml)	baking soda
¾ tsp (4 ml)	salt
1 cup (250 ml)	sugar
½ cup (125 ml)	chopped pecans
1¾ cups (425 ml)	low-fat buttermilk
¾ tsp (4 ml)	vanilla extract
¾ tsp (4 ml)	almond extract

1 Preheat the oven to 450°F (230°C). Lightly flour a baking sheet.

2 In a large bowl, whisk together the spelt flour, baking soda, salt and sugar. Stir in the pecans. In a medium bowl, stir together the buttermilk and extracts. Add the wet ingredients to the dry mixture and give it a quick stir just to combine—don't overmix.

3 Turn the dough out onto the baking sheet and form it into a ball. Flip it over. Using a steak knife, cut an X across the top of the dough, about ¼ inch (5 mm) deep and slightly deeper in the middle. Bake for 15 minutes. Lower the temperature to 400°F (200°C) and bake for another 25 minutes, or until golden brown. Transfer to a rack and allow to cool completely. Store in an airtight container for up to a week or freeze for up to a month.

SWEET POTATO CHIPS WITH YOGURT DIPPING SAUCE

Despite having a mother who gravitates toward sweet flavors, Scarlett prefers savory just like her potato-chip-obsessed father. It's all I can do to keep bags of the classic snack from piling up in my pantry like I'm a corner convenience store. One way is to always have these crisp chips on hand. Her dad misses his bowl of mindless enjoyment, but Scarlett loves having a chip that comes with its own dipping sauce. **LK**

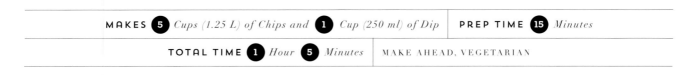

MAKES ⑤ *Cups (1.25 L) of Chips and* ① *Cup (250 ml) of Dip*	**PREP TIME** ⑮ *Minutes*
TOTAL TIME ① *Hour* ⑤ *Minutes*	MAKE AHEAD, VEGETARIAN

2	sweet potatoes
2 Tbsp (15 ml)	olive oil
1 tsp (5 ml)	sea salt

HONEY YOGURT DIPPING SAUCE

1 cup (250 ml)	plain Greek-style yogurt
1 tsp (5 ml)	honey
¼ tsp (1 ml)	ground cinnamon

> **TIP** See a photo of our Sweet Potato Chips with Yogurt Dipping Sauce on page 16.

1. Preheat the oven to 350°F (180°C). Line a baking sheet with parchment paper.

2. Using a knife, vegetable slicer or mandoline, slice your sweet potatoes into super-thin slices of equal thickness.

3. In a medium bowl, whisk together the oil and salt. Add the potato slices and toss until coated.

4. Arrange potato slices, in a single layer and not overlapping, on the baking sheet. Bake for 50 minutes, turning once or twice, until the edges are a dark golden brown and the centers are cooked throughout. Keep a watchful eye on the chips, as they can burn quickly. (This is the only instance where you should break the rule of thumb to never open the oven. I find that allowing some heat to escape when I check the chips keeps them from burning but allows the centers to cook through.) Allow the chips to cool on the baking sheet. They will crisp up even further as they cool.

5. For the dipping sauce, stir together the yogurt, honey and cinnamon. Serve chips with dipping sauce. Store chips in a resealable plastic bag for up to 3 days. Store dipping sauce in the refrigerator.

BANANA AND STRAWBERRY LOAF

Sweet strawberries add texture and a little novelty to this classic banana bread, and just a slice makes a perfect after-school snack. Add a glass of milk for the kids, and a cup of coffee for you. **CM**

MAKES 1 *Loaf*	**PREP TIME** 15 *Minutes*	**TOTAL TIME** 1 *Hour* 10 *Minutes*	MAKE AHEAD, VEGETARIAN

1	egg
1 cup (250 ml)	mashed ripe bananas (about 2 large bananas)
½ cup (125 ml)	brown sugar
½ cup (125 ml)	plain Greek-style yogurt
¼ cup (60 ml)	vegetable oil
1 tsp (5 ml)	vanilla extract
1 cup (250 ml)	all-purpose flour
½ cup (125 ml)	whole wheat flour
1 tsp (5 ml)	ground cinnamon
1 tsp (5 ml)	baking soda
1 tsp (5 ml)	baking powder
¼ tsp (1 ml)	salt
½ cup (125 ml)	chopped strawberries
3 or 4	strawberries, sliced

> **TIP** Do you have brown, soft bananas on your counter? Those are the ones you want in this loaf! If you don't have time to bake when your bananas are perfectly ripe, just peel them, toss them into a freezer bag and get them in the freezer. Then just pull them out when you're ready.

1. Preheat the oven to 350°F (180°C). Lightly grease a loaf pan.

2. In a large bowl, lightly beat the egg, then mix in the mashed bananas, sugar, yogurt, oil and vanilla. In a medium bowl, whisk together the all-purpose flour, whole wheat flour, cinnamon, baking soda, baking powder and salt. Add the dry ingredients to the wet and stir just until they're combined. Don't overmix or you'll end up with tough bread. Stir in the chopped strawberries until they're mixed evenly throughout the batter.

3. Pour the batter into the loaf pan. Arrange the strawberry slices across the top of your loaf. Bake for 45 to 55 minutes, until the bread is golden brown and a toothpick inserted in the center comes out clean. Allow the loaf to cool for a few minutes before turning it out onto a rack to cool completely. Store in an airtight container or wrapped in plastic wrap for up to 1 week.

PUMPKIN AND CRANBERRY LOAF

Consider this loaf banana bread's fall counterpart. I love the tartness of the cranberries against the creamy sweetness of the pumpkin. Although it's filled with nutritious ingredients, the smell of this coming out of your oven will have your kids thinking you're making dessert, not a healthy snack. **CM**

MAKES **1** *Loaf*	PREP TIME **15** *Minutes*	TOTAL TIME **1** *Hour* **5** *Minutes*	MAKE AHEAD, VEGETARIAN

1½ cups (375 ml)	whole wheat flour
1 tsp (5 ml)	salt
1 tsp (5 ml)	baking soda
½ tsp (2 ml)	ground cinnamon
½ tsp (2 ml)	grated nutmeg
¼ tsp (1 ml)	ground ginger
2	eggs
1 cup (250 ml)	pumpkin purée
½ cup (125 ml)	brown sugar
⅓ cup (75 ml)	vegetable oil
¼ cup (60 ml)	orange juice
1 cup (250 ml)	fresh cranberries

TIP You can substitute frozen cranberries for fresh. Just be sure to thaw them first and drain off excess moisture before using.

1. Preheat the oven to 350°F (180°C). Lightly grease a loaf pan.

2. In a large bowl, whisk together the flour, salt, baking soda, cinnamon, nutmeg and ginger. In another large bowl, using an electric mixer, mix the eggs, pumpkin purée, sugar, oil and orange juice until well combined. Shake the dry ingredients over the wet in three additions, stirring between each addition until just combined. Stir in the cranberries.

3. Pour the batter into the loaf pan and use a spatula to smooth the top a bit. Bake for 50 minutes, or until a toothpick inserted in the center comes out clean. Allow the loaf to cool for about 15 minutes before turning it out onto a rack to cool completely. Store in an airtight container or wrap in plastic wrap and refrigerate for up to 1 week.

BROWNIE BITES

This recipe represents my love-hate relationship with dessert. I don't want my kids eating too much sugar or growing up with the expectation that every meal should end with a sugary finish. But chocolate calls to me in the same way it does to them. Short of eating it under cover of darkness once they're in bed (I would never!), I like these teeny, supremely decadent brownie bites. As dessert or a mid-afternoon treat, they're wildly satisfying to kids and adults alike. **CM**

| **MAKES** 30 *Cookies* | **PREP TIME** 30 *Minutes* | **TOTAL TIME** 1 *Hour* | MAKE AHEAD, VEGETARIAN |

1½ cups (375 ml)	all-purpose flour
¼ cup (60 ml)	cocoa powder
¾ tsp (4 ml)	baking soda
½ tsp (2 ml)	salt
½ cup (125 ml)	butter, room temperature
½ cup (125 ml)	brown sugar
½ cup (125 ml)	maple syrup
1½ cups (375 ml)	roughly chopped semisweet chocolate
¼ cup (60 ml)	granulated sugar

TIP Don't let the tiny size of these bites fool you. They deliver big time on chocolatey-ness.

1. In a large bowl, mix together the flour, cocoa powder, baking soda and salt.

2. In a separate bowl and using an electric mixer, cream the butter with the brown sugar until it's light and fluffy, about 3 minutes. Add the maple syrup and beat again until well combined. With the mixer on low speed, gently shake in your flour mixture bit by bit. Add the chocolate and beat again until it all comes together. Cover and refrigerate for 30 minutes or overnight.

3. Preheat the oven to 325°F (160°C). Line a baking sheet with parchment paper.

4. Spread the granulated sugar on a plate or work surface. Using a teaspoon, scoop the dough generously and roll it between your hands to make balls. Now roll those balls around in the sugar to coat them. Place on the baking sheet, leaving about 1 inch (2.5 cm) between the cookies.

5. Bake for 9 minutes, or until the cookies just begin to crack and are set. Allow to cool for a few minutes, then transfer to a rack to cool completely. Store in an airtight container for up to 1 week.

BLUEBERRY GRUNT GREATNESS

One summer weekend, we visited our friends the Murphys at their cottage. With rain teeming down, we found ourselves inside filling our time with board games, dance parties and baking. Our most memorable kitchen project was Doug's blueberry grunt. A traditional dessert from the East Coast of Canada, this bowl of happiness was impossible to stop eating even after the rain-battered cottage sprung a leak over our heads. With the memory of our time in the kitchen, I created this replica of our rainy-day treat. If you've never enjoyed a grunt's warm, soupy blueberry sauce topped with slightly sweetened biscuits, then you need to try this recipe. And, of course, it tastes better if you share it with special friends. **LK**

MAKES **6** *Servings*	PREP TIME **15** *Minutes*	TOTAL TIME **30** *Minutes*	VEGETARIAN

4 cups (1 L)	fresh or frozen blueberries
½ cup (125 ml)	sugar
½ cup (125 ml)	water
2 tsp (10 ml)	lemon zest
½	lemon, juiced

DUMPLINGS

2 cups (500 ml)	spelt flour
1 Tbsp (15 ml)	baking powder
1 tsp (5 ml)	sugar
½ tsp (2 ml)	salt
¼ tsp (1 ml)	ground allspice
¼ cup (60 ml)	cold butter
1¼ cups (300 ml)	milk, more if necessary

TIP This dessert is only made better by the addition of vanilla bean ice cream.

1. In a deep 9-inch (23 cm) skillet, mix the blueberries, sugar, water, lemon zest and lemon juice. Bring to a boil, then reduce heat and simmer for 5 minutes.

2. Meanwhile, for the dumplings, sift the flour, baking powder, sugar, salt and allspice into a large bowl. Using a pastry cutter or two knives, cut in the butter until the mixture looks like coarse crumbs. Mix in the milk using a fork until the dough comes together. (You may need to drizzle in a bit more milk, as the dough is very dry.)

3. Drop heaping tablespoons of the dough onto the berries. Cover with a lid or foil and cook dumplings until they puff up, are cooked in the center and are lightly brown, 12 to 15 minutes. Serve warm.

TIP These are bake sale all-stars!

CHOCOLATE CHIP COOKIE BARS

There are some things in life you can bank on. Like, you're never going to find out about your kid's school's bake sale earlier than the night before. Ever. No worries—these quick and easy bars are going to become your go-to (for last-minute or long-lead bake sales). They pack up easily without disintegrating, they're cute and they're crazy good. We don't care what the committee says, these are worth $1.50 a piece. **CM**

MAKES **24** *Bars*	PREP TIME **10** *Minutes*	TOTAL TIME **40** *Minutes*	MAKE AHEAD, VEGETARIAN

¾ cup (175 ml)	butter, melted
½ cup (125 ml)	brown sugar
2	eggs
2 tsp (10 ml)	vanilla extract
2 cups (500 ml)	whole wheat flour
½ tsp (2 ml)	baking soda
½ tsp (2 ml)	salt
1 package (12 oz/340 g)	chocolate chips
½ cup (125 ml)	unsweetened shredded coconut

1. Preheat the oven to 350°F (180°C). Line a 13- by 9-inch (3 L) baking pan with parchment, leaving a bit of overhang on each long side to help you lift your bars out later.

2. In a medium bowl, whisk together the melted butter, sugar, eggs and vanilla until the mixture is creamy and light. In a large bowl, whisk together the flour, baking soda and salt. Slowly stir in the wet ingredients until just combined. Mix in the chocolate chips and the coconut. Don't overmix or you'll have tough bars!

3. Scrape the mixture into the baking pan. Bake for 25 to 30 minutes, until a toothpick inserted in the center comes out clean. Cool in the pan for a few minutes before lifting the cookie out and cutting into 24 rectangular bars. Allow to cool completely. Store in an airtight container for up to 1 week.

STRAWBERRY AND BANANA NICE CREAM

I never shied away from giving Scarlett ice cream. Despite the sugar, I adopted an "everything in moderation" motto because I was a fan of the summer treat's calcium. Until I met Nice Cream. I may never go back to regular ice cream, especially since I can mix dark chocolate shavings right into this recipe. Forget you read that. **LK**

MAKES **4** *Servings*	PREP TIME **5** *Minutes*	TOTAL TIME **1** *Hour* **5** *Minutes*	MAKE AHEAD, VEGETARIAN

3 cups (325 ml)   frozen strawberries
2   frozen bananas
1 cup (250 ml)   almond milk
½ cup (125 ml)   Greek-style yogurt
2 Tbsp (30 ml)   almond butter

1. Place strawberries, bananas, milk, yogurt and almond butter in a blender. Whiz until smooth.

2. Pour into a medium bowl and pop into the freezer for 1 hour. Scoop and enjoy.

LEMON RICOTTA COOKIES

These cookies are perfect. Except that they're so soft and light you can hardly be blamed for needing to eat three in a row. (Or four—who's counting?) Their cakey texture and zingy glaze only make them worse. I mean better. **CM**

MAKES 30 *Cookies*	**PREP TIME** 20 *Minutes*	**TOTAL TIME** 40 *Minutes*	MAKE AHEAD, VEGETARIAN

1 cup (250 ml)	sugar
2½ Tbsp (37 ml)	lemon zest (about 2 lemons)
½ cup (125 ml)	butter, room temperature
1	egg
2 cups (500 ml)	ricotta cheese
¼ cup (60 ml)	lemon juice
1 tsp (5 ml)	vanilla extract
2 cups (500 ml)	all-purpose flour
1 tsp (5 ml)	baking powder
½ tsp (2 ml)	salt

GLAZE (OPTIONAL)

1 cup (250 ml)	confectioners' sugar
1 Tbsp (15 ml)	lemon zest (about 1 lemon)
3 Tbsp (45 ml)	lemon juice

1. Preheat the oven to 350°F (180°C). Line two baking sheets with parchment paper.

2. In a large bowl, mix the sugar and lemon zest. Use your fingers to work the zest thoroughly into the sugar. Add the softened butter and, using an electric mixer, beat until light and fluffy, 2 or 3 minutes. Add the egg, ricotta, lemon juice and vanilla and beat again until the mixture is very smooth.

3. In another bowl, whisk together the flour, baking powder and salt. Shake the dry ingredients over the wet in two additions, gently folding in each addition just until combined.

4. Drop level tablespoons of batter onto the baking sheets, about an inch (2.5 cm) apart from each other. Bake for 20 minutes in the middle of the oven, or until cookies are set but just barely golden. Transfer cookies to racks and allow to cool completely.

5. To glaze, place the racks over the used baking sheets to catch the drips. In a small bowl, whisk together the glaze ingredients. Drizzle the glaze over the cookies. Allow the glaze to set before serving. Store in an airtight container for up to 1 week.

LEMON CARDAMOM APPLE CAKE

This cake was created to tick off a lot of boxes for our families. First, Ceri and I wanted a simple, not-too-sweet sheet cake that could be dressed up for entertaining. But we also wanted something featuring fresh fruit that could be eaten for breakfast or with an afternoon coffee. This cake not only delivered but also met another unexpected need: it quickly became my neighborhood kids' most requested after-school nibble. There is also rumor of it going to school as a snack and standing up to the terror of the backpack, never to be traded. **LK**

| **MAKES** 16 *Servings* | **PREP TIME** 15 *Minutes* | **TOTAL TIME** 50 *Minutes* | MAKE AHEAD, VEGETARIAN |

3	Gala or Fuji apples, peeled and cut into ½-inch (1 cm) cubes
½ tsp (2 ml)	ground cinnamon
1 cup (250 ml)	spelt flour
1 cup (250 ml)	finely ground cornmeal
1 cup (250 ml)	sugar
1½ tsp (7 ml)	baking powder
1½ tsp (7 ml)	baking soda
¼ tsp (1 ml)	ground cardamom
¼ tsp (1 ml)	salt
2	eggs
½ cup (125 ml)	applesauce
¼ cup (60 ml)	lemon juice
2 Tbsp (30 ml)	vegetable oil
1 tsp (5 ml)	vanilla extract
⅔ cup (150 ml)	buttermilk

TIP See a photo of this cake on page 168.

1. Preheat the oven to 350°F (180°C). Butter an 11- by 7-inch (2 L) glass baking dish.

2. In a bowl, toss the apple cubes with cinnamon. Arrange them in the baking pan. Set the bowl aside.

3. In a large bowl, whisk together the flour, cornmeal, sugar, baking powder, baking soda, cardamom and salt. Using the bowl from the apples, whisk together the eggs, applesauce, lemon juice, oil and vanilla. Pour the wet ingredients into the dry and stir. Add the buttermilk and stir until just combined. Pour the batter over the apples.

4. Bake for 35 minutes, or until a toothpick inserted in the center comes out clean. Allow to cool, then cut into squares. Store in an airtight container for up to 1 week.

When the last teacher gift has been bestowed and report cards are in, that means it's time for cake.

PEPPERMINT PATTIES

I realize I'm asking you to make candy here, but the smooth and minty coconut-and-cashew middles of these patties make up for the fact that they're coated in chocolate and considered the "C" word. And forget about the kids. After a long, stressful day, one of these little buttons of pleasure is better to me than a glass of wine. That's no lie. **LK**

MAKES **30** *Patties*	PREP TIME **15** *Minutes*	TOTAL TIME **1** *Hour*	MAKE AHEAD, VEGETARIAN

1 cup (250 ml)	unsweetened shredded coconut
1 cup (250 ml)	unsalted and unroasted cashews
2 tsp (10 ml)	peppermint extract
1 Tbsp (15 ml)	honey
1 Tbsp (15 ml)	coconut oil, melted
½ lb (225 g)	70% dark chocolate, sliced into shavings

1 In a food processor, pulse the coconut and cashews until you have a fine meal. Add the peppermint extract, honey and coconut oil and process until combined.

2 Lay out two square sheets of plastic wrap. Divide the coconut mixture into halves and tip each half onto a sheet of plastic wrap. Roll the mixtures into two logs about 1 inch (2.5 cm) thick. Twist the ends of the logs to seal. Place in the freezer for 30 minutes.

3 Melt the chocolate in a heatproof bowl placed over (not in) a pot of simmering water. Once the chocolate is half melted, remove the bowl from the pot and continue stirring until the rest of the shavings melt. Return the bowl to the pot to keep the chocolate from hardening, but remove it from the stove.

4 Line two baking sheets with parchment paper. Unwrap the coconut logs and slice them into ¼-inch (5 mm) rounds. Using a slotted spoon, dunk the rounds one at a time in the melted chocolate, being sure to coat them on both sides. Tap off excess chocolate and then place the rounds on the baking sheet. Place the baking sheets in the freezer for about 15 minutes, until the chocolate sets. Store in an airtight container in the freezer for up to 2 months. (That's a joke! You can't possibly make them last that long.) Remove from freezer 15 minutes before you'd like to enjoy them so they soften.

ACKNOWLEDGMENTS

Creating a cookbook is a shocking amount of work. But it's also a wonderful process, especially if you're lucky enough to work with a brilliant team. We have been so lucky; everyone who touched this book made it better and more fun to work on.

We're so grateful to the team at Penguin Random House of Canada and Appetite. Thank you to Kristin Cochrane for your ongoing support, to Robert McCullough for your faithful friendship and guidance, to Martha Kanya-Forstner for just getting it from the very beginning, to Scott Richardson for always making the pages better than we imagined, to Shaun Oakey for the eagle-eyed copy edits, to Susan Burns for making sure the book actually became a book, and to Trish Bunnett for helping us get this labor of love out into the world. And a special thank you to the beautiful Bhavna Chauhan, whose dedication, thoughtfulness, enthusiasm and care made each step of this book's development a damn joy. We love you, girl!

Big love for the production crew of this baby. We're so lucky to have worked again with brilliant photographer, genius collaborator and loyal friend, Maya Visnyei. Thank you for taking anything we throw at you with such ease, care and grace. Every image in this book was improved by food stylist David Grenier's stunning, thoughtful work (and those high kicks didn't hurt either). Thanks to prop stylist Catherine Doherty, whose incredible taste and devoted friendship make everything in our world prettier. Thanks to Leila Ashtari, Carmen Cheung, Tristan Knowlton, Zach Koski, James Reiger, Cara Tegler and Ashley Van Der Laan for helping in too many ways to mention, and to dietician Cara Rosenbloom for her nutritional wizardry.

A million thanks to Yhony Munoz for letting us shoot in your home before you even moved in. You are a prince! And our appreciation to Laura Lanktree for jumping in on this project, and for being an all-around great friend to SPC.

Sincere thanks to everyone at The McDermid Agency, especially Anne and Chris for their continued support.

We send love and appreciation to all the families that taste-tested and road-tested recipes, as well as shared with us their frustrations and successes with cooking through the school year, including the Cihras, Coutts, Dickinsons, Ewarts, Hodgsons, Mackenzies, Murphys, Nobbs, Pypers and Sharpe-Temples.

And, most importantly, we are so grateful to the readers of sweetpotatochronicles.com and *How to Feed a Family*. Thank you for allowing SPC to be a part of your homes' kitchens. This is all for you.

FROM LAURA: To Scarlett, for always eating your lunch and being the most willing and fun companion in the kitchen. To Dan, for happily devouring all those failed recipes, and being so darn proud. To Brian, for being a one-man, PR powerhouse. Thank you to all my friends and family for your infinite excitement, love and support of everything SPC, especially my mom and dad, who don't remember a thing about having a kid in school but thought this book was the bee's knees anyway. I love you.

FROM CERI: To Esme and Julian, thanks for your patience through the less fun aspects of cookbook creation (recipe testing again?) and your enthusiasm for the really fun parts (photo shoots!)—there's no one I'd rather pack lunches for. I'm grateful to my whole family for their encouragement, but mostly to Ben for everything you do for our family.

INDEX